Victor Pankratius, Samuel Kounev (eds.)

Emerging Research Directions in Computer Science

Contributions from the Young Informatics Faculty in Karlsruhe

Emerging Research Directions in Computer Science

Contributions from the Young Informatics Faculty in Karlsruhe

Victor Pankratius
Samuel Kounev
(eds.)

Impressum

Karlsruher Institut für Technologie (KIT)
KIT Scientific Publishing
Straße am Forum 2
D-76131 Karlsruhe
www.uvka.de

KIT – Universität des Landes Baden-Württemberg und nationales
Forschungszentrum in der Helmholtz-Gemeinschaft

KIT Scientific Publishing 2010
Print on Demand

ISBN 978-3-86644-508-6

Preface

It is my pleasure to introduce this volume outlining new directions in computer science investigated by the junior researchers of the faculty of informatics at the Karlsruhe Institute of Technology (KIT). Each paper presents a young researcher's scientific contributions and the research vision for a whole junior research group.

All junior groups play a very important role at our faculty, and the junior research group leader positions are all roughly equivalent to assistant professors. As the term "junior researcher" is not yet standardized in Germany, our groups are supported through different instruments, such as junior professorships, shared research groups, young investigator groups, junior research groups, and the Emmy-Noether program. Consequently, the funding sources vary as well: we would like to thank the excellence initiative at KIT, the German Science Foundation (DFG), the Tschira-Stiftung, as well as several companies, namely Harmann-Becker, Init and PTV, for their generous support of young scientists.

The faculty of computer science is doing a lot to attract young talents. It offers all junior researchers a high degree of autonomy and support to lead their groups independently, including the same authorization as the full tenured professors to award doctoral degrees. They also have direct support from the faculty board, the dean, and a dedicated mentor for consultation.

I think that all statements contained in this volume present high-quality, innovative research. We are very proud that these young outstanding researchers are part of KIT!

Prof. Dr. Ralf Reussner
Vice Dean of the Faculty of Informatics
Karlsruhe, Germany
May 2010

Table of Contents

Image and Video Analysis to Enable Human-Friendly Systems

Rainer Stiefelhagen

Institute for Anthropomatics
Karlsruhe Institute of Technology
and
Fraunhofer Institute of Optronics, System Technologies
and Image Exploitation (IOSB), Karlsruhe
rainer.stiefelhagen@kit.edu

Abstract. In order to build better human-friendly human-computer interfaces, such interfaces need to be enabled with capabilities to perceive the user, his location, identity, activities and in particular his interaction with others and the machine. Only with these perception capabilities can smart systems – for example human-friendly robots or smart environments – become posssible. In my research I'm thus focusing on the development of novel techniques for the visual perception of humans and their activities, in order to facilitate perceptive multimodal interfaces, humanoid robots and smart environments. My work includes research on person tracking, person identification, recognition of pointing gestures, estimation of head orientation and focus of attention, as well as audio-visual scene and activity analysis. Application areas are human-friendly humanoid robots, smart environments, content-based image and video analysis, as well as safety- and security-related applications. This article gives a brief overview of my ongoing research activities in these areas.

1 Introduction

With the increasing performance of today's computers and their entry in all areas of our lives and society, user-friendly and intuitive "human-centered" interaction between humans and computers becomes a necessity.

To make the vision of human-centered systems – such as human-friendly robots, or smart supportive envrionments – possible, such systems need to be able to perceive humans, their locations, identities, actions, and so on. In my research I'm thus focusing on the development of novel computer vision techniques for the automated visual perception of humans. My work includes for example research on person tracking, person identification, recognition of pointing gestures, estimation of head orientation and focus of attention, as well as audio-visual scene and activity analysis. Currently the main application scenarios I am working on are human-friendly humanoid robots, smart environments, content-based image and video analysis, as well as security-related applications.

This research is supported in the framework of a so-called shared professorship on "Computer Vision for Human-Computer Interaction (CV-HCI)" which was granted to me beginning of May 2009. The position is funded partially by the Karlsruhe Institute of Technology - where I lead a research group with the same name within the Institute for Anthropomatics - as well as by the Fraunhofer Institute for Optronics, System Technologies and Image Exploitation (IOSB), in Karlsruhe, where I also direct the research group "Perceptual User Interfaces".

In the remainder of this article, I will give a brief overview of our research on visual perception of humans in order to build human-friendly robots (Section 2), to build smart perceptive and supportive environments (Section 3), as well as on content-based image and video analysis (Section 4). The paper is concluded by a summary and outlook (Section 5).

2 Human-Robot Interaction

For a humanoid robot, the perception of the users, their locations, identities, gestures, and other communicative cues is an essential necessity for efficient and safe interaction. It allows the robot to understand what users want, and to generate an appropriate response. As a member of the Sonderforschungsbereich SFB588 "Humanoid Robots" [14] we are working on the visual perception capabilities of a humanoid robot [1] with respect to the user and his activities.

In the framework of this project we have for example developed an integrated real-time person tracking system capable of localizing multiple people in the field-of-view of the robot's stereo camera[8,7]. The tracking is based on the dynamic combination of multiple cues and can cope with partial occlusion as well as with deficiencies of single features.

Once a person is localized, his or her identity is estimated by means of face recognition, and the person's focus of interest is determined by means of head-pose estimation [13]. The user's hands are tracked in 3D, and pointing gestures are detected based on gesture models that have been learned from hundreds of training gestures [9]. These components provide necessary cues to enable multi-modal interaction with the humanoid robot [16].

Currently, our work related to human-robot interaction focuses on the automatic recognition of activities of daily living, especially of activities performed in the kitchen. To this end, we investigate both appearance and model-based approaches for action and activity recognition.

The idea is to enable a robot ways to acquire brief knowledge about what is going on in a room shortly after he entered the room. This way, the robot can easily adapt to the room situation and react accordingly. After identifying that somebody is unloading the dishwasher, the robot could for instance offer his help or even take over the task without any need of explicit commands.

To recognize activities automatically, we use the fact that human activities can be discriminated to a certain degree by their single motions even under different environmental conditions. Also the existence of some tools involved in an activity contains information about the activity itself. For instance, it is very likely that a person performing an activity with a knife is cutting something. However, instead of developing a new classifier for each object and each motion type, we use both kinds of information implicitly by employing low-level image-based features like motion and image-gradients to classify a situation.

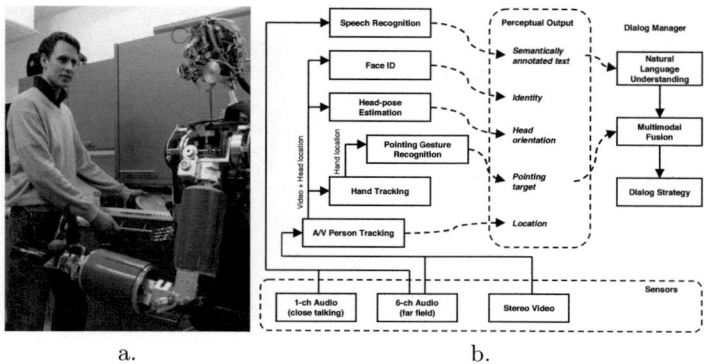

a.   b.

Fig. 1. Interaction with the humanoid robot Armar-III[1] (a.) and overview of the perception components. The visual perception components include person tracking, hand tracking and pointing gesture recognition, head pose estimation and face recognition. Also components for speech recogntion, natural language understanding and dialog processing are included, allowing for a multimodal interaction with the robot (joint work with A. Waibel et al., see [16]).

Another ongoig activity is markerless human body tracking which shall be employed for the recognition of single actions and gestures. Similar to techniques used in costly movie-productions, human body motions are to be captured but without requiring the user to wear special clothes or interacting in a blue-/green-screen environment. Instead, we are investigating methods to track a simplified articulated body model with the need of only a single stereo-camera sensor.

Because computational resources of a robot are limited by the low amount of available space and because they need to be shared among multiple components like speech-recognition or robot control modules, particular attention has to be paid to a real-time capability of the investigated methods.

3   Smart Environments

As smart environments one can consider sensorized environments that can perceive the users and their activities in it, and which aim at supporting these users during their activities in these rooms. Examples are smart houses, smart meeting rooms or smart lecture rooms.

I have extensively worked on building perceptual technologies for smart environments, including smart offices, meeting and lectures rooms [19,4,15,2,18,20].

An example application for a smart office is the so-called Connector service. This service uses perception components in and in front of an office to determine the current activity inside the office, and uses this information to handle incoming phone calls in a context-specific way. In a user study we could show that this lead to significantly reduced number of disruptions while still preserving caller-satisfaction[3].

Building a smart room to support crisis control is currently the main focus of my research conducted at the Fraunhofer Institute for Optronics, System Tech-

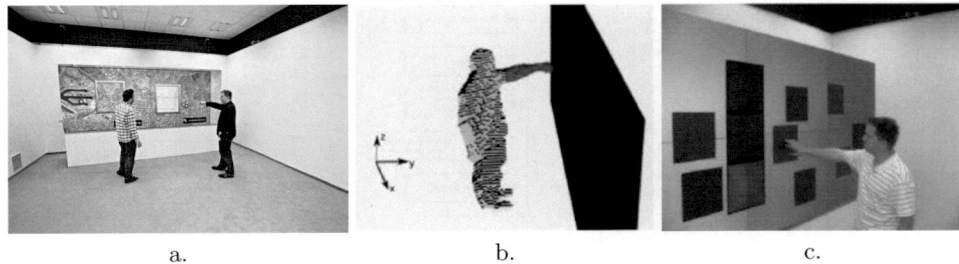

a.   b.   c.

Fig. 2. The IOSB Smart Control Room laboratory, containing a videowall and cameras (a.). Using cameras in the smart room, the visual hull of people in the room can be extracted in real time (b.). By extracting the 3D arm pose and hand position of users in front of the video wall, pointing and touch-based interaction becomes possible (c.).

nologies and Image Exploitation [6]. There, we aim at building a "smart control room" in which we use audio-visual perception to support team collaboration and to facilitate multimodal interaction with large displays.

Our experiments take place in a laboratory of six by nine meters, equiped with a number of cameras and with a large video-wall.

By analyzing the video-streams captured with the cameras, we are able to perceive the identities, locations, head orientations, body pose and gestures of the people in the room in real-time. The 3D-analysis of body pose and gestures is then used to allow for an intuitive touch- and pointing-based interaction with the video-wall [12,11].

In the framework of this project we also work on high-level analysis of the situation in the smart room. To this end we currently investigate the use of temporal logic to fuse the outputs of low-level perception modules in order to get a higher-level interpretation of the scene. Our longterm goal is to be able to provide automatic reports of what is going on the smart room.

4 Content-Based Image and Video Analysis

With the increasing amount of available multimedia data, it has become more and more important to be able to automatically analyze multimedia content and retrieve it according to the user's wishes. There are many technologies involved in such a task. First of all, the content of the multimedia data should be represented in a suitable way to facilitate successful retrieval. This requires the use of audio-visual and text analysis tools to derive descriptions of the multimedia data. Afterwards, the search can be conducted either in a fully automatic way or in an interactive way by adding the user to the decision loop.

As a member of the French-German project Quaero [10], we are working on visual and multimodal analysis of multimedia content. Here, our contributions include detection, localization and identification of people in multimedia content, as well as multimodal recognition of high-level features, genres and events.

Within the Quaero project, we have developed a robust and very efficient face and facial feature detector as well as systems for filtering image search results, for finding actors in movies and TV shows, for recognition of video genres and for the detection of concepts in videos. Figure 3 shows a screenshot of a system we developped for interactive actor retrieval [5].

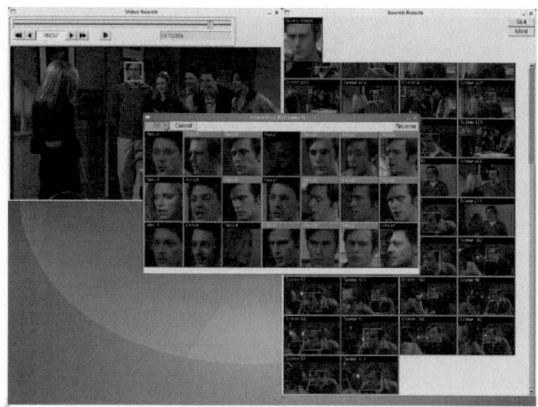

Fig. 3. Screenshot from our system for interactive actor retrieval [5]. The user can search for scenes with a specific actor by clicking on the face of an actor in one scene (upper left window). Search results (right window) can then interactively be refined by marking correct and false results from a number of additional suggestions given by the system (window in front).

Interactive search for persons is also relevant for security-related applications. It can for example be applied to finding specific people in live or stored recordings coming from a distributed camera network. This could for example be useful to determine where a specific (suspicious) person has come from, and where it has been going since it has been observed in a specific view. In addition to face recognition, we also investigate the use of other cues for re-identification, such as features describing a person's clothing and knowledge about the sensor topology [17] (see Figure 4).

5   Summary and Outlook

This paper has given a brief overview of my ongoing research activities. The main goal of my research is to develop methods to enable smart systems that can perceive and intelligently interact with human users. To this end we are working on novel methods to detect and track humans, to identify them, to analyze their body poses, gestures and actions, their head pose and facial expressions. The goal is to provide better and better perception capabilities to machines. This also includes the fusion and aggregation of "low-level" perception into higher-

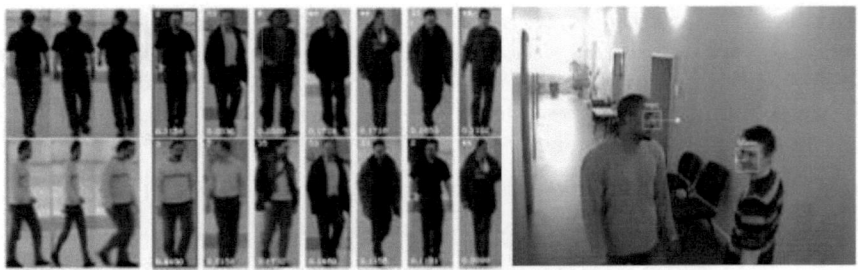

Fig. 4. Person re-identification on the basis of clothing features. The first three images on the left are sample views of a person to be recognized among a set of possible persons. The result of the system is a ranking of possible matches, ordered by the probability of a correct match from left to right. The red boxes around the persons show that in fact the correct persons were identified. (right) Identification and head pose estimation. By tracking faces over non-frontal head-poses, it is possible to correctly identify persons even when they do not directly look into the camera.

level perception and situation analysis, an area in which yet a lot of research has to be done in the coming years.

In addition to working on the better perception capabilities, it is also important to address how to make the best use of machine perception in order to provide really useful, intuitive and user-friendly human-computer interfaces. To this end, complete end-to-end real-time systems have to be built, and user studies need to be conducted.

Computer vision-based perception of humans has a large number of important application areas. Some of the applications we currently address include human-friendly robots, smart environments (in particular a smart crisis control-room), content-based image and video analysis (e.g. retrieval of actors or other people in images and video) and security related applications (e.g. person identification for access control, person localization and re-identification in camera networks). In the framework of a new project, we have also started working on visual monitoring of patients in order to improve patient safety in hospitals and nursery homes. But there are many more relevant application areas, including driver-assistant systems (awareness of the driver and passengers, as well of humans outside a car), assistive systems for handicapped people, and in principle any type of system where humans are involved.

Acknowledgments

This research has been partially funded by the DFG under Sonderforschungs-bereich 588 "Humanoid Robots", by OSEO, France, under the Quaero programm, by the the Fraunhofer Gesellschaft under Internal Programm Grant No. 692026 (Attract), by the BMBF under the projects GEMS (Gesture Based Human Computer Interaction in Emergency Management Systems) and VIPSAFE (Automated Visual monitoring for Improving Patient SAFEty).

References

1. T. Asfour, K. Regenstein, P. Azad, J. Schröder, A. Bierbaum, N. Vahrenkamp, and R. Dillmann. ARMAR-III: An integrated humanoid platform for sensory-motor control. In *IEEE-RAS International Conference on Humanoid Robots (Humanoids 2006)*, Genoa, Italy, December 2006.
2. K. Bernardin, R. Stiefelhagen, and A. Waibel. Probabilistic integration of sparse audio-visual cues for identity tracking. In *Proceedings of ACM Multimedia 2008*, Vancouver, BC, Canada, 2008.
3. M. Danninger and R. Stiefelhagen. A context-aware virtual secretary in a smart office environment. In *Proceedings of ACM Multimedia 2008*, Vancouver, BC, Canada, 2008.
4. H. K. Ekenel, M. Fischer, Q. Jin, and R. Stiefelhagen. Multimodal person identification in a smart environment. In *CVPR Biometrics Workshop 2007, IEEE Conference on Computer Vision and Pattern Recognition*, Minneapolis, USA, 2007.
5. Mika Fischer, Hazim K. Ekenel, and Rainer Stiefelhagen. Interactive person re-identification in tv series. In *8th International Workshop on Content-Based Multimedia Indexing*, Grenoble, France, 2010.
6. Research Group Perceptual User Interfaces at Fraunhofer IOSB, http://www.iosb.fraunhofer.de//servlet/is/20718/.
7. K. Nickel and R. Stiefelhagen. Dynamic integration of generalized cues for person tracking. In *10th European Conference on Computer Vision - ECCV'08*, Marseille, France, 2008.
8. Kai Nickel and Rainer Stiefelhagen. Fast audio-visual multi-person tracking for a humanoid stereo camera head. In *IEEE-RAS 7th International Conference on Humanoid Robots - Humanoids'07*, Pittsburgh, PA, 2007.
9. Kai Nickel and Rainer Stiefelhagen. Visual Recognition of Pointing Gestures for Human-Robot Interaction. *Image and Vision Computing*, 25(12):1875–1884, 2007.
10. Quaero Program. http://www.quaero.org.
11. A. Schick and R. Stiefelhagen. Real-time gpu-based voxel carving with systematic occlusion handling. In *Proceedings of the 31st Symposium of the German Association for Pattern Recognition (DAGM)*, Jena, Germany, 2009.
12. A. Schick, F. van de Camp, J. Ijsselmuiden, and R. Stiefelhagen. Extending touch: Towards interaction with large-scale surfaces. In *Proceedings of Interactive Tabletops and Surfaces 2009*, Banff, Canada, 2009.
13. E. Seemann, K. Nickel, and R. Stiefelhagen. Head Pose Estimation Using Stereo Vision for Human-Robot Interaction. In *Sixth International Conference on Face and Gesture Recognition - FG 2004*, Seoul, Korea, May 2004. IEEE.
14. Sonderforschungsbereich 588 Humanoide Roboter - Lernende und kooperierend multimodale Roboter. http://www.sfb588.uni-karlsruhe.de/.
15. J. Stallkamp, H. K. Ekenel, and R. Stiefelhagen. Video-based face recognition on real-world data. In *Int. Conference on Computer Vision - ICCV'07*, Rio de Janeiro, Brasil, 2007.
16. R. Stiefelhagen, H. Ekenel, C. Fügen, P. Gieselmann, H. Holzapfel, F. Kraft, K. Nickel, M. Voit, and A. Waibel. Enabling Multimodal Human-Robot Interaction fort the Karlsruhe Humanoid Robot. *IEEE Transactions on Robotics*, 2007. to appear.
17. F. van de Camp, K. Bernardin, and R. Stiefelhagen. Person tracking in camera networks using graph-based bayesian inference. In *Proceedings of the Third ACM/IEEE International Conference on Distributed Smart Cameras (ICDSC)*, Como, Italy, 2009.

18. M. Voit and R. Stiefelhagen. Tracking Head Pose and Focus of Attention with Multiple Far-field Cameras, International Conference on Multimodal Interfaces. In *International Conference on Multimodal Interfaces*, pages 281–286, Banff, Canada, November 2006. ACM.

19. Alex Waibel and Rainer Stiefelhagen, editors. *Computers in the Human Interaction Loop*. Human-Computer Interaction Series. Springer, 2009.

20. C. Wojek, K. Nickel, and R. Stiefelhagen. Activity Recognition and Room-Level Tracking in an Office Environment. In *IEEE Int. Conference on Multisensor Fusion and Integration for Intelligent Systems - MFI06*, Heidelberg, Germany, September 2006.

Short Biography

Dr. Rainer Stiefelhagen is a professor of Computer Science at the Karlsruhe Institute of Technology, where he is directing the research field on "Computer Vision for Human-Computer Interaction". He is also head of the research field "Perceptual User Interfaces" at the Fraunhofer Institut for Optronics, System Technologies and Image Exploitation (IOSB) in Karlsruhe. His research focuses on the development of novel techniques for the visual and audio-visual perception of humans and their activities, in order to facilitate perceptive multimodal interfaces, humanoid robots and smart environments. In 2007, Dr. Stiefelhagen was awarded one of currently five German Attract projects in the area of Computer Science funded by the Fraunhofer Gesellschaft. His work has been published in more than one hundred publications in journals and conferences. He has been a founder and Co-Chair of the CLEAR 2006 and 2007 evaluation workshops (Classification of Events, Activities and Relationships) and has been Program Committee member and co-organizer in many other conferences. He is a standing committee member of the ACM International Conference on Multimodal Interfaces (ICMI) and of the Workshop on Multimodal Interaction and Related Machine Learning Algorithms (MLMI). He is also member of the editorial board of the Springer Journal on Multimodal Interfaces. He is co-founder of Videmo Intelligente Videoanalyse GmbH & Co. KG, a Karlsruhe based company developing innovative software for intelligent video analysis, with a focus on applications related to security and customer monitoring. Dr. Stiefelhagen received his Doctoral Degree in Engineering Sciences in 2002 from the Universität Karlsruhe (TH).

Contact Information

Prof. Dr.-Ing. Rainer Stiefelhagen
Institute for Anthropomatics
Karlsruhe Institute of Technology
Adenauerring 2, Geb. 50.20.
76131 Karlsruhe
Phone: +49 721 608 6385
Email: rainer.stiefelhagen@kit.edu
URL: http://cvhci.ira.uka.de

Advanced technical cognitive systems for mobility assistance

J. Marius Zöllner[1,2], Thomas Schamm[2], Dennis Nienhüser[2], Thomas Gumpp[2],
Florian Steinhardt[2], Tobias Bär[2], Marcus Strand[2], Ralf Kohlhaas[2]

[1] KIT, Karlsruher Institute of Technology, Germany
[2]FZI Forschungszentrum Informatik, Karlsruhe, Germany
Marius.Zoellner@kit.edu
{zoellner, schamm, nienhueser, gumpp, steinh, baer, strand, kohlhass}@fzi.de

Abstract. Mobility for persons becomes one of the biggest needs in our daily life. It covers different modes like regional mobility, local area mobility and different goals like fast, comfortable, affordable or efficient mobility. Within this field, intelligent technical systems can provide assistance for different applications. Advanced driver assistance systems up to semi-autonomous individualized mobility systems are addressed by our research.
Key issues characterizing technical cognitive systems for advanced assistance are perception, interpretation of the environment, the situation and the user, probabilistic situational reasoning and also learning.

Keywords: intelligent vehicles, cognitive systems, mobility, advanced driver assistance, service robotics, fusion, probabilistic inference

1 Introduction

One of the main mobility providing systems are intelligent cars equipped with driver assistance systems for safety, comfort or energy efficiency. Today's driver assistance systems can support the user during simple driving tasks (for a good overview see [1]). However, these systems are rather limited to special tasks and for instance still not able to decide whether and how a driver needs support.
For the development of next generation advanced driver assistance systems (ADAS) a need for complex environment perception and interpretation exists. As example, not only the current driving lane or the nearest obstacle are of importance, but also the whole environment including neighboring lanes as well as other obstacles or traffic rules have to be considered. Additionally, reasoning about the current environmental situation and the prediction of its development must be fulfilled. Also recognition of the user, his intention and behavior are mandatory to provide user-adaptive assistance. Skills of an intelligent co-driver addressed by our current research include risk estimation and in future risk reduction but also comfortable and user adaptive energy efficient driving. Our work addresses also the future integration of semi-autonomous driving skills like a so-called "guardian angel" for emergency situation [18].

Future city mobility concepts will contain in addition personalized mobile systems. One important role will be played by autonomous and semi-autonomous transportation platforms. The need for individual public transportation platforms for urban environments led to the development of new vehicle concepts in the last years. Autonomous city vehicles like the Cybercars [2] provide an approach to reduce the number of private vehicles in inner city areas but are limited to car-friendly environments. Our SegIT transporter (see fig. 7) is a new mobile platform based on a Segway PT, customized for car-adverse urban areas like the city center or large indoor rooms like exhibitions or shopping malls.

Similar to intelligent ADAS the SegIT transporter is intended as a transportation platform with user adaptive assistance.

As a further assistance concept we consider autonomous robots providing support in local areas like shopping centers. One such demonstrator is our InBot robot. In addition to already mentioned perceptive and interpretations skills, the autonomous behavior in cooperation with the user is addressed within this context [17].

All above mentioned systems have in common that starting from a reliable perception, an interpretation of the environment and the user under uncertainties, probabilistic inference and based on this reliable action decision define the technical cognitive assistance system.

This paper presents exemplarily some of our achievements within this scope, whereby the main focus lies on advanced driver assistance systems.

Perception, Fusion, Interpretation and Reasoning for ADAS

In the following methodical key aspects of our work within environment perception and interpretation, user interpretation and probabilistic situation evaluation are briefly described. Further details on road detection, sign and additional signs detection, signpost detection, evidence based information fusion, object detection but also the ADAS evaluation within a virtual driving test can be found in [3-12].

Environment perception and knowledge fusion

A great amount of background knowledge for ADAS comes through digital maps built into nearly ubiquitous navigation systems. In addition, the on-road recognition of different environment components like speed and additional signs, lanes, construction sites etc. become affordable and extend the knowledge of the system.

One of the main challenges is the extraction of relevant information – the situation context – and its incorporation into a reliable fusion process. For example, for a reliable speed limit information system among the relevant recognized entities are the presence of variable message signs, the presence of road works, the weather conditions and the daylight.

Besides the recognition of different entities (see [5][9][11]), in [7] we have proposed a novel approach of fusing digital background information and online extracted information (see fig. 1). Core of the fusion is a Dempster-Shafer approach wherein by the use of adaptive, so-called mass functions, based on the perceived situation context the belief and thus the influence of different knowledge sources are carried out.

Fig. 1. Vision based system are beneficial in the presence of construction sites and dynamic traffic signs, while digital maps are preferable in bad weather and adverse lighting scenarios. Adapting sensor input reliability in such situations improves fusion results.

Qualitative evaluations show promising results: The fusion is able to determine the speed limit in situations where either a digital map or a camera-based system alone would fail. Additionally, the situation context awareness shows clear benefits as it is able to reduce the number of conflicting situations compared to a fusion process not using this information. Furthermore this concept allows performing a probabilistic perception defining the confidence of the result, a principle that we use also for detection of drivable areas like roads or temporarily roads in construction sites [6].

The comprehension of dynamic objects in the environment is a major concern of predictive assistance systems, in order to improve safety and comfort functions, like the well-known adaptive cruise control. Furthermore, for partly autonomous systems knowledge of the surrounding environment is needed to select appropriate driving behaviors or to perform proper path planning. Not only the detection of objects but also the recognition of their maneuver state and this in different conditions, during daytime, bad weather and at night are required.

Existing work in vehicle detection uses different sensors from monocular video sensors up to active sensors (lidar, radar sensors) or promising depth based sensors, like time-of-flight cameras. The major impact comes through the fusion of appearance-based methods like symmetry, shadow or trained classifiers, taking full advantage of previous knowledge about objects with active sensor data.

Besides promising results showed in [10][8] in [4] we present a novel approach for low feature-level data fusion of disparities in u-disparity-space (see fig. 2) and preprocessed radar data. By this an increase of around 11,8% compared with the single use of 2-D data could be achieved.

A still existing challenge is the vehicle detection under darkness, especially during dusk and at night (see fig. 2). Our approach based on three major steps uses as core an iterative sensor preprocessing, adaptive Gaussian filter and a probabilistic hypothesis generation [3]. Within this available model knowledge about symmetry but also color information is used. Thus it is able to distinguish between the front and rear position lights and the breaking maneuver state of the vehicles.

Fig. 2. Left: Example for u/v-disparity-space labeled with object-type. The color scale shows the area of u/v-disparity to which a point with corresponding color of the disparity image will be mapped. Right: Rear lights and breaking light detection of a vehicle and a truck (above) and oncoming vehicles during dusk and at night.

Experiments done on more than 5000 image frames, comparing the detection rate of the system show very promising results for both dusk and night illumination situations. The ongoing work on hypothesis verification evaluating classification methods for vehicle candidates will enhance the performance even on dark image sequences. Illumination changes of the position lights are also topic of ongoing research, especially to detect the activity of turn light indicators.

Among the relevant objects we consider not only static information and dynamic road users, but also semi-static parts of the traffic infrastructure like traffic lights switching their state and thus changing the situation. Not only for comfort application, informing the user in case of bad visibility but especially for safety, informing the user about unseen red lights and (semi) autonomous maneuver preventing crashes or optimizing fuel consumption at intersections due to turning on and off the engine, full knowledge about the traffic situation is required.

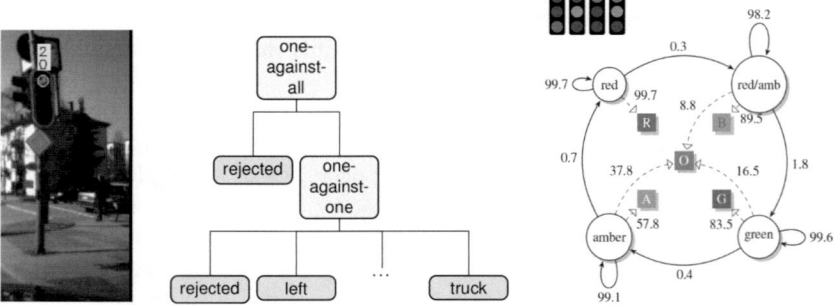

Fig. 3. Traffic lights (left) can be recognized and tracked with classification rate by cascades of support vector machines (middle) in combination with hidden Markov Models for temporal fusion and state estimation (right).

Obviously successful application must achieve very high true positive rate, avoiding false positives and false negatives. Our approach by using morphological operations and rule based filters for segmentation and combining multiple support vector machine cascades for classification with hidden Markov models for temporal fusion as well as state estimation (see fig. 3) proved to be a valuable contribution towards this goal. The system is able to detect, track and recognize several traffic lights simultaneously with a classification rate of more than 91%.

Within the perception process learning occurs a priori on the different processing levels. The next step will be to learn to predict states and state changes on specific traffic situations.

Driver Perception and interpretation

User adaptive assistance requires knowledge about the driver. Within this context one major issue is the estimation of the focus of attention of the driver. Thus both, the head pose estimation and the gaze tracking are relevant. Therefore we are using two methods, a tome-of-flight estimation of the head pose and an appearance based tracking of the drivers eyes. The core methods use an adaptive head model tracked by probabilistic feature extraction like eye-corner, mouth etc in 3D and 2D data, supported by the optical image flow and a iris detection in the extracted eye region (see fig. 4).

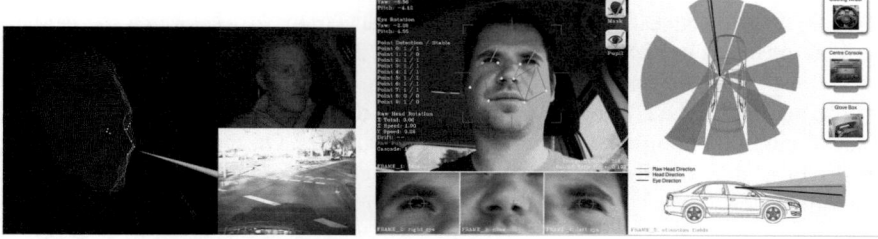

Fig. 4. Headpose estimation based on 3D tof data (left) and appearance based gaze tracking and focus of attention detection (right).

Based on the detection result due to a temporal fusion a classification of the focus of attention within 12 x3 regions of interest including the surrounding of the car but also the internal areas of the car is performed. In order to improve the estimation currently a driver model based on typical driving maneuvers is evaluated. Further work will address the learning of the drivers behavior in different situations and the prediction of his intention. Together with the probabilistic situation interpretation (described below) this should lead to more advanced but also reliable assistance.

Probabilistic Situation Interpretation – exemplarily for Risk Assessment

Commonly used definitions of risk define the risk as the product of the probability of a hazard event and the severity of the event. Assuming that the term which can be measured an influenced primarily by an ADAS is the accident's probability, it is necessary to develop probabilistic methods which able to estimate the risk given the environmental situation and the driver's state.

Focusing on methods flexible, extendable, able to incorporate background knowledge and which can handle uncertainty our approach is based on the concept of object-oriented probabilistic relational model (OPRM) language. An OPRM is a probabilistic relational representation, which combines first-order probabilistic languages with Bayesian inference. The OPRM is defined by two components, a relational component and a probabilistic component. While the relational component describes the relations between classes in the domain, the probabilistic part describes the dependencies between attributes of the classes.

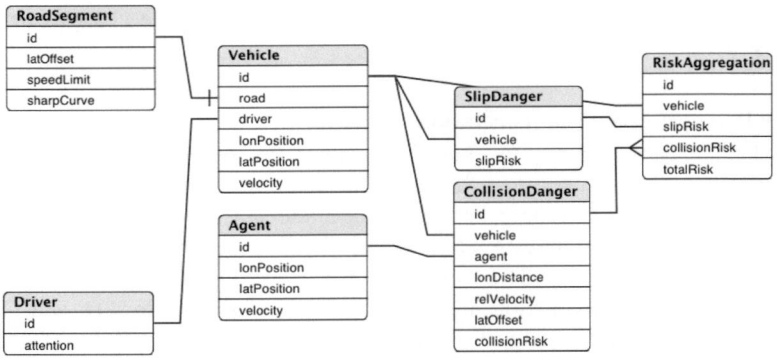

Fig. 5. A simple relational model for the driver assistance domain. The overall risk depends on relations (on the right side) between OPRM classes.

On the one hand, the risk of a driving situation depends on the relations between the vehicle and other entities, e.g. agents or road segments. On the other hand, as long as the driver is able to influence the vehicle, the overall risk is influenced by the driver's attention.

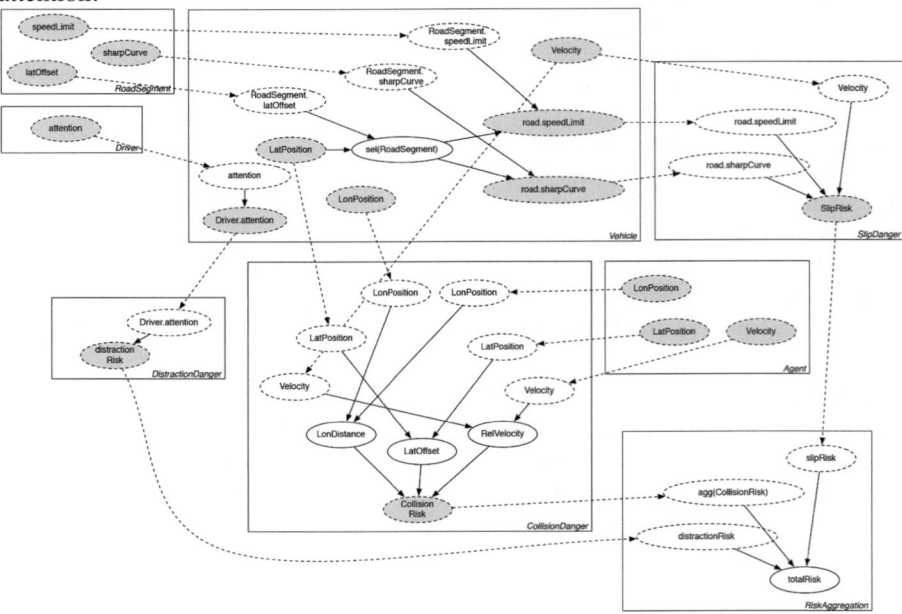

Fig. 6. Resulting OOBN combining the collision, slip and user distraction risks.

Common driving situations may include possible collisions between the ego vehicle and other vehicles, or the slip danger due to a speed limit violation in sharp curves. The risk of both situations however is affected by the attention of the driver. A simple relational model covering this example is shown in fig 4.

The major advantage using OPRM is that there exists an underlying object-oriented Bayesian network, which can dynamically be created and evaluated on runtime. The corresponding OOBN for the risk assessment described above can be seen in fig. 5.

It can be shown that neglecting the users attention this approach expands common collision estimation approaches, like the time-to-collision value based approach. Using this concept the perception and interpretation can be integrated into a well-grounded high-level framework of reasoning.

Conclusion and Further work in the domain of ADAS
The used concept with probabilistic perception and information fusion and probabilistic inference based on OPRM is reliably and performs very good. Furthermore it is expandable to more than risk assessment. Current work addresses reasoning for energy efficiency but also for semi-autonomous maneuver generation within this framework.

Besides improving situation interpretation the next steps of our research will concentrate on adaptivity and learning. As a basis the already mentioned OPRMs will be used. Learning will include both, the structural aspect (setting up the relational models for different reasoning tasks) but also the probabilistic dependencies between attributes. Another important topic addressed in future will be the backward inference and thus the estimation of useful supporting actions for the driver.

Personalized mobility systems – SegIT

Personalized technical systems providing especially individual and safe navigation assistance are key issues for future mobility. As concept mobility systems we set up the *SegIT* transporters (fig. 7) intended to provide augmented navigation assistance like informing about traffic rules or predictably planning collision-free paths and partially able to navigate (semi) autonomously. The latter will be used for instance to perform safety movements while driven by the user or to move completely autonomous to a static or dynamic target point for picking up persons demanding for transport.

Beside control issues (see []) and the 2D/3D perception sensor system, including sensor data preprocessing ([]), and the extraction of drivable terrain and objects [], within the development of such high end robotic systems, directly cooperating in human centered environments, one major challenge is to make them adaptable to dynamic environments.

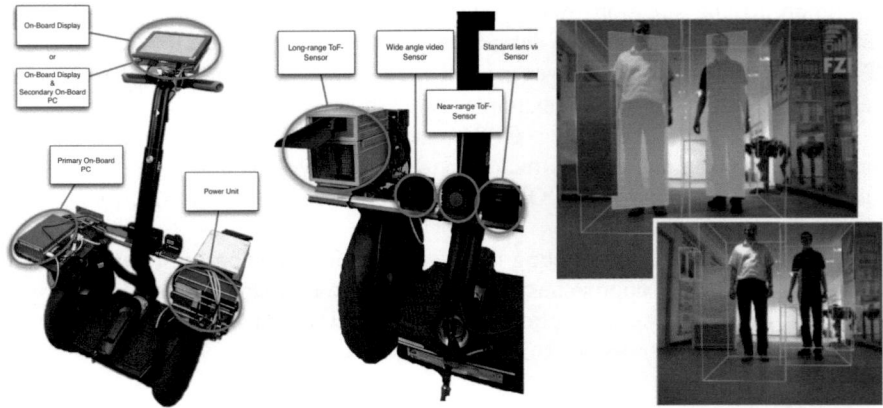

Fig. 7. SegIT transportation platform. On-Board PCs, human-machine interface and power unit (left) provides augmented navigation support based on 3D and 2D sensors (middle). Object detection and classification is done by information fusion (right).

Thus, to achieve more robust object detection the time of flight based object detection has been enhanced with an appearance-based region classification. This approach is based on environment models that consist of rectangular planes representing objects in the world. Using statistical knowledge, point clouds of the tof camera are segmented into 3D planes. Textures of flat objects are extracted for eased pattern segmentation. Resulting planes are classified with monocular detection algorithms and object dimensions are refined. Thus, using for instance wavelet-based Adaboost cascades we achieve good result in people detection and by isometric texture extraction good classification results on sign recognition.

Future work in the area of personalized mobility systems will extend the object detection approach by a Kalman Filter to achieve temporal fused information. IMM tracking filter will be considered as well especially in order to differentiate between static and dynamic object.
Based on this we will enhance the drivable path generation with the reactive methods already used successful for the InBot assistance Robot, which rely on the prediction of object paths and combine different strategies, like escape dynamic objects or retreat from dynamic objects with classical path planning. For details please refer to [15][16]. Another major key aspect will be shared control consisting of the fusion of the navigation behaviors with the predicted users intention.

Acknowledgment

The work presented here was partially supported by the KIT, the FZI, Harman Becker Automotive GmbH, the EU (contract number IST-045441) and the Ministry of Economic Affairs of Baden-Württemberg.

References

1. H. Winner, S. Hakuli und G. Wolf: Handbuch Fahrerassistenzsysteme, Grundlagen, Komponenten und Systeme für aktive Sicherheit und Komfort Wiesbaden: Vieweg+Teubner Verlag 2009, ISBN 978-3-8348-0287-3
2. C. Pradalier, J. Hermosillo, C. Koike, C. Braillon, P. Bessire, and C. Laugier. The CyCab: a car-like robot navigating autonomously and safely among pedestrians, Robotics and Autonomous Systems, 50(1):51-68, 2005
3. T. Schamm, C. von Carlowitz, and J. M. Zöllner: On-Road Vehicle Detection during Dusk and at Night, IEEE Intelligent Vehicles Symposium 2010, San Diego, USA (to appear)
4. M. Teutsch, T. Heger, T. Schamm, and J. M. Zöllner 3D-Segmentation of Traffic Environments with U/V-Disparity supported by Radar-given Masterpoints, IEEE Intelligent Vehicles Symposium 2010, San Diego, USA (to appear)
5. D. Nienhüser, T. Gumpp, J. M. Zöllner and K. Natroshvili: Fast and Reliable Recognition of Supplementary Traffic Signs, IEEE Intelligent Vehicles Symposium 2010, San Diego, USA (to appear)
6. T. Gumpp, D. Nienhüser, R. Liebig and J. M. Zöllner: Recognition and tracking of temporary lanes in motorway construction sites, IEEE Intelligent Vehicles Symposium 2009
7. D. Nienhüser, T. Gumpp and J. M. Zöllner: A Situation Context Aware Dempster-Shafer Fusion of Digital Maps and a Road Sign Recognition System, Intelligent Vehicles Symposium 2009
8. T. Schamm, J. M. Zöllner, S. Vacek, J. Schröder, R. Dillmann: Obstacle detection with a Photonic Mixing Device-camera in autonomous vehicles, International Journal of Intelligent Systems Technologies and Application, Volume 5, Issue ¾, pp 315-324, 2008
9. D. Nienhüser, T. Gumpp, J. M. Zöllner, R. Dillmann: Recognition and Attribution of Variable Message Signs and Lanes, IEEE Intelligent Vehicles Symposium (IV'08), Eindhoven, Holland
10. Vacek S., Schamm T., Schröder J., Zöllner J.M., Dillmann R.: Collision avoidance for cognitive automobiles using a 3D PMD camera, Intelligent Autonomous Vehicles 2007, Toulouse, France
11. Nienhüser D., Ziegenmeyer M., Gumpp T., Scholl K.-U., Zöllner J.M., Dillmann R.: Kamera-basierte Erkennung von Geschwindigkeitsbeschränkungen auf deutschen Straßen, Autonome mobile Systeme (AMS 2007), 18-19 Oktober, Kaiserslautern, Deutschland
12. M. Ziegenmeyer, D. Nienhüser, T. Schamm, T. Gumpp, T. Bär, J. M. Zöllner, J. Henning, B. Schick: Durchgängige Evaluierung von Verfahren zur Informationsfusion für bildgestützte Fahrerassistenzsysteme mit Hilfe einer Umgebungs- und Fahrsimulation, 4. Tagung Sicherheit durch Fahrerassistenz, April, München 2009
13. M. Strand, T. Schamm, A. Benazza, T. Kerscher, M. Zöllner, R. Dillmann: Control of an autonomous personal transporter towards moving targets, IEEE Workshop on Advanced Robotics and its Social Impacts (ARSO), Tokyo, Japan, November 2009
14. T. Schamm, M. Strand, T. Gumpp, R. Kohlhaas, J. M. Zöllner, R. Dillmann: Vision and ToF-based driving assistance for a personal transporter, 14th International Conference on Advanced Robotics (ICAR 2009), Munich
15. M. Göller, F. Steinhardt, T. Kerscher, J.M. Zöllner and R. Dillmann: Reactive Avoidance of Dynamic Obstacles using the Behavior Network of the Interactive Behavior-Operated Shopping Trolley InBOT, 12th International Conference on Climbing and Walking Robots and Support Technologies for Mobile Machines (CLAWAR09)
16. M. Göller, T. Kerscher, J.M. Zöllner, R. Dillmann: Obstacle Handling of the holonomic-driven Interactive Behavior-Operated Shopping Trolley InBOT, IEEE Seventh International Workshop on Robot Motion and Control (RoMoCo09)

17. M. Göller, F. Steinhardt, T. Kerscher, J.M. Zöllner, R. Dillmann: Robust Navigation System Based on RFID Transponder Barriers for the Interactive Behavior-Operated Shopping Trolley InBOT, Volume 4, Issue 36 of the international Journal Industrial Robot, Emerald Group Publishing Limited
18. Semi-autonomous automobiles, FZI, http://www.fzi.de/index.php/en/research/strategic-research/taa

J. Marius Zöllner is professor at the Institute for Anthropomatics at the Computer Science Faculty of the Karlsruher Institute of Technology (KIT). He is also Director of Technical Cognitive Assistance Systems at the Forschngszentrum Informatik FZI.
His main research interests include: Machine Learning and probabilistic Inference, Robotics and Intelligent Vehicles

Marcus Strand is post doctoral researcher and department manager of the Technical Cognitive Assistance Systems group at the Forschungszentrum Informatik FZI. His main research interests include: autonomous robots, mobile IT navigation and localization

Dennis Nienhüser is researcher at the group Technical Cognitive Assistance Systems at the Forschungszentrum Informatik FZI. His main research interests include: intelligent vehicles, machine learning, machine vision, information fusion

Thomas Schamm is researcher at the group Technical Cognitive Assistance Systems at the Forschungszentrum Informatik FZI. His main research interests include: intelligent vehicles, 2D/3D object recognition, reasoning

Thomas Gumpp is researcher at the group Technical Cognitive Assistance Systems at the Forschungszentrum Informatik FZI. His main research interests include: intelligent vehicles, image processing, tracking

Tobias Bär is researcher at the group Technical Cognitive Assistance Systems at the Forschungszentrum Informatik FZI. His main research interests include: intelligent vehicles, user and situation interpretations

Florian Steinhardt is Ph.D student in the group Technical Cognitive Assistance Systems at the Forschungszentrum Informatik FZI. His main research interests include: robotics, path planning, behavior based control

Ralf Kohlhaas is researcher at the group Technical Cognitive Assistance Systems at the Forschungszentrum Informatik FZI. His main research interests include: intelligent vehicles, probabilistic action selection

The Internet in Your Hand – Chances and Challenges of Creating Service Overlays on Mobile and Heterogeneous Devices

Oliver P. Waldhorst

Institute of Telematics, Karlsruhe Institute of Technology (KIT), Karlsruhe, Germany
waldhorst@kit.edu

Abstract. Accessing applications from mobile devices significantly increases the pervasiveness of the Internet. Service overlays are a novel paradigm for service provisioning that seems well suited to support this vision. However, mobile devices impose new challenges by increasing heterogeneity as well as mobility induced dynamics, that hinder development and deployment of service overlays. This chapter shows how the young investigator group *Controlling Heterogeneous and Dynamic Mobile Grid and Peer-to-Peer Systems* (*CoMoGriP*) faces these challenges and provides the building blocks to foster creation of service overlays.

1 Introduction

As a pervasive tool for private and professional communication the Internet is an important part of our daily life. It provides various services including sending e-mails, chatting, browsing the World Wide Web, exchanging files, and making telephone calls. The increasing dependency on the Internet implies an increase in non-functional requirements, e. g., availability, robustness, and security. New and emerging applications have new functional requirements, e. g., efficient content distribution among groups of users. In particular the trend towards "always-connected" applications on mobile devices like the iPhone calls for mechanisms supporting mobility of users and devices. In fact, the Internet must constantly keep up with these challenges by providing new protocols and services. Unfortunately, deploying new protocols and services on a global scale is difficult due to various technical and non-technical reasons.

An convenient way to integrate new services into the Internet comprise *overlay-networks* (or for short *overlays*). Overlays in general enable service provisioning on top of a existing infrastructure (usually denoted as *underlay*). To this end, an overlay links devices and systems physically connected to the underlay by logical connections. Thus, it establishes a topology that is independent of the actual underlay. Many overlays provide a customized addressing scheme and create virtual networks on top of the physical network.

In the last years, a particular type of overlays, so called *peer-to-peer* (*P2P*) systems, gained significant importance. P2P systems implement new functionality by *service overlays* that solely connect devices at the edge of the Internet, e. g., personal computers, notebooks, or smart phones as shown in Figure 1. Thus, they do not require any changes to the established Internet infrastructure. The devices connected by the overlay

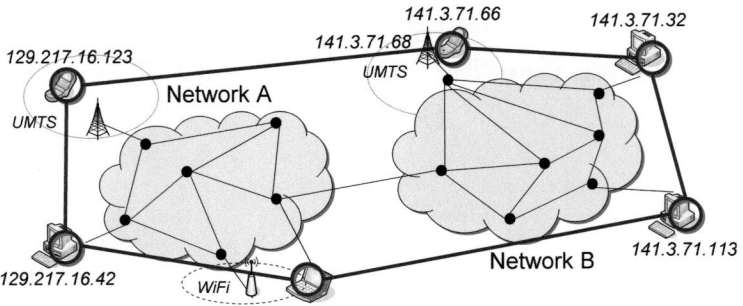

Fig. 1. An overlay connecting heterogeneous an partially mobile devices.

provide resources such as network bandwidth or storage for implementing an overlay-based service. Following [13], a P2P overlay requires *fault tolerance*, *self-organization*, and *massive scalability* as fundamental properties. Fault tolerance is required since a device is not always available and, e. g., may leave the overlay without prior notice. Self-organization is essential since all devices in a P2P system are equal with respect to their role in the overlay. In particular, each end-system must be able to integrate into the overlay and perform its task based on locally available information. Since there exist P2P systems comprising (ten) millions of nodes, massive scalability is mandatory.

Popular examples of P2P systems include file sharing platforms like BitTorrent and telephone services like Skype. Their success undeniably proves that service overlays constitute a driving force for innovation in the Internet. But despite all these appealing features, the construction of service overlays is not easy in face of an evolving Internet. In particular, the integration of mobile devices into overlays raises new challenges by increasing the level of mobility-induced dynamics, the number of multi-homed devices due to simultaneous connections by several network technologies, as well as the heterogeneity of protocols, access-networks, and devices [17].

To this end the Young Investigator Group *Controlling Heterogeneous and Dynamic Mobile Grid and Peer-to-Peer Systems* (*CoMoGriP*) provides tools that ease the development and deployment of service overlays in an evolving Internet. Figure 2 depicts CoMoGriP's mayor working areas in this scenario. The remainder of this chapter describes challenges and solutions within each of the mayor working areas. Section 2 describes how a generic overlay-architecture can foster development and deployment of service overlays. A particular challenge for such architecture is maintaining connectivity in face of of devices moving between heterogeneous networks, as discussed in Section 3. Furthermore, the initial integration of a mobile device into an existing overlay imposes several challenges that are discussed in Section 4. We present a group communication service offering multicast capabilities as an example for a service overlay in Section 5. Section 6 shows how the energy consumed by service provisioning can be controlled in order to foster the acceptance of mobile device owners. Finally, concluding remarks are given.

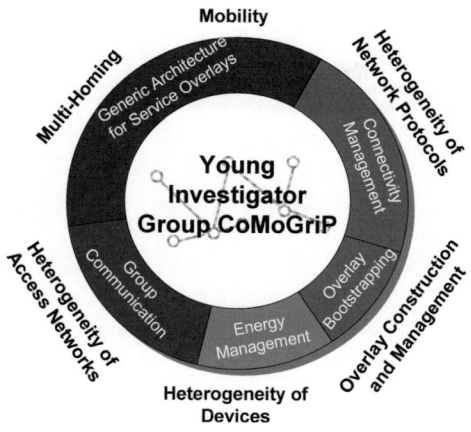

Fig. 2. Working areas of the Young Investigator Group *Controlling Heterogeneous and Dynamic Mobile Grid and Peer-to-Peer Systems (CoMoGriP)*

2 An Overlay-based Service Architecture

Many popular P2P systems provide solutions to a subset of the challenges imposed by an evolving Internet with mobile devices. For example, some systems include mechanisms to reconnect a device that moves between different access networks to the overlay. Nevertheless, such mechanisms are likely tailored to a particular P2P system and reuse in other P2P systems is hardly possible.

A mayor goal of CoMoGriP is to enable easy overlay construction by identifying mayor building blocks and providing them as a generic and reusable toolkit. To this end, an architecture for the flexible creation of service overlays is developed within the *Spontaneous Virtual Networks (SpoVNet)* project [16]. This architecture, denoted as *SpoVNet architecture*, avoids manual configuration and implements self-organization by using overlays on several layers as shown in Figure 3. Beside consequently building applications and services based on overlays, the architecture itself relies on overlays for providing its mayor functionality. For that purpose, the *SpoVNet base* uses an overlay to provide device connectivity (cmp. Section 3) based on a uniform and persistent addressing scheme. It implements SpoVNet's *underlay abstraction layer* [1] that hides the obstacles of the mobile and heterogeneous network from the service overlay developer, who can, thus, solely focus on implementing service functionality. We have shown that easy service creation is in fact possible using *ariba*, a prototype implementation of the SpoVNet-base [10]. Furthermore, within the SpoVNet-framework, multiple example services have been implemented, including a group communication serivce (cmp. Section 5) and an event notification service. The interfaces to these services comprise SpoVNet's *service abstraction layer*, that is designed to hide changes in the service implementation from the applications. E. g., when a future version of the Internet supports native multicast, this can easily replace the functionality of the group communication service.

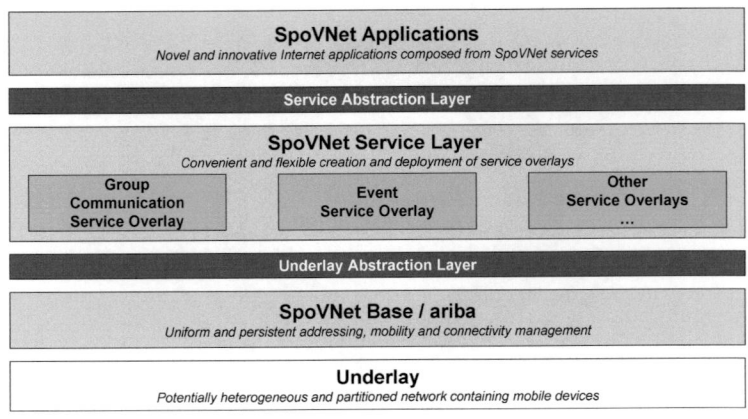

Fig. 3. The Spontaneous Virtual Networks (SpoVNet) architecture.

Current work focuses on providing generic building blocks besides basic connectivity that allow for composition of customized service overlays, significantly reducing development efforts. Furthermore, support for upcoming concepts like virtualized networks and the "Internet of things" is integrated.

3   Providing Overlay Connectivity

One major goal of the SpoVNet architecture is to provide connectivity. In fact, an evolving Internet faces a sneaking loss of end-to-end connectivity due to several reasons [15]: First, *Network Address Translation*—commonly used in home DSL and cable routers—causes that overlay connections to some devices cannot be established directly. Second, the partial upgrade to IPv6—the next version of the Internet protocol—results in devices running different protocol versions, which cannot establish connections without manual configured translation mechanisms. Third, moving a mobile device between different access networks implies breaking overlay connections.

CoMoGiP develops tools to provide overlay connectivity despite the obstacles described above *without manual configuration*. Figure 4 depicts an example scenario comprising two networks A and B. Network B runs IPv6, whereas Network A still uses the older version of the Internet protocol, IPv4, indicated by the different format of the addresses next to the devices. A device that is connected to both networks (Device 2) can establish overlay connections to any other device in both networks. However, establishing an overlay connection between devices in different networks (e. g., the dashed connection between Device 1 and 3) is only possible if the data flow is directed through a *relay device* connected to both networks (Device 2), using two separate overlay connections.

To enable self-organizing discovery and construction of such overlay connections, we have proposed a protocol for detecting overlay partitions and relay devices [14]. Furthermore, we have successfully demonstrated the capability of the ariba prototype

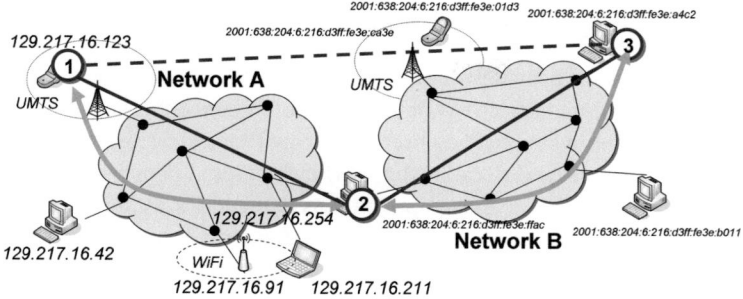

Fig. 4. Relay devices enable overlay connections across heterogeneous networks.

implementation of the SpoVNet base to transparently establish and maintain overlay connections in scenarios as depicted in Figure 4 [7, 8]. Current work includes the development of mechanisms that can cope with increased dynamics such as splitting and merging of networks. Furthermore we design scalable routing mechanisms for forwarding messages between heterogeneous networks across the overlay.

4 Overlay Bootstrapping

Besides providing connectivity despite of the network obstacles described above, constructing a service overlay requires mechanisms to initially connect a (mobile) device. Such mechanisms typically require the new device to establish a connection to at least one device that is already active in the overlay. Many mechanisms for the initial connection procedure (usually denoted as *bootstrapping*) require support of dedicated (centralized) infrastructure for maintaining lists of currently active devices contradicting the principle of self-organization.

To avoid this dependency on infrastructure, CoMoGriP develops mechanisms for decentralized, self-organizing bootstrapping within the *Communication by Autonomous Infrastructures* (*Kommunikation mittels Autonomer Infrastrukturen, KAI*) project. We showed that re-joining an overlay even after several hours of inactivity is feasible by maintaining a list of formerly active devices in a *local host cache* [3]. Unfortunately, this is infeasible after long periods of disconnection and in particular for first-time users. Thus, we proposed an approach for discovering an active devices without any a-priori information, given a P2P overlay of reasonable size. We showed that in IPv4 networks randomly probing for active peers in address spaces allocated to dial-up networks leads to a success within a few minutes for the popular BitTorrent P2P system [3]. However, we also found that limitations typical DSL hardware as well as behavior of BitTorrent peers hinders faster bootstrapping by this approach, and proposed ways to speed up the procedure [3]. Although random probing seems to be infeasible for IPv6 networks due to the much larger address space, structural properties of IPv6 addresses combined with anycast capabilities can help to make bootstrapping possible [2]. Current work includes implementation and prototype based evaluation of these mechanisms.

5   Group Communication as Example Services

Beside providing tools for easy development and deployment of service overlays, Co-MoGriP itself also develops service overlays as a proof of concept. The use case considered in this context is motivated by the observation that IP multicast is a technology that has been developed for several decades, but still lacks global deployment for reasons that are manifold. Nevertheless, many applications demand for multicast communication in face of current trends towards video and TV transmission. Thus, implementing a group communication service that provides multicast capabilities is a ideal use-case for service overlays. The functionality implemented by such service overlay is usually denoted as *application layer multicast (ALM)*.

CoMoGriP analyses the potential and drawbacks of application layer multicast with respect to the challenges imposed by mobile and heterogeneous networks. We analyzed the performance of ALM mechanisms when distributing data to a large, heavily fluctuating number of receivers [11]. Furthermore, we showed that adapting overlay parameters at run-time is an appropriate tool to cope with network dynamics [9]. The group communication service implemented in the SpoVNet architecture (cmp. Section 2) builds upon the lessons learned from these studies. It exploits the different properties of various communication technologies available at mobile devices in order to maximize user-perceived performance and minimize network load, as shown by the example of WiFi networks [12]. In current work this concept is extended to other technologies.

6   Controlling Energy Consumption

Beyond the context of service overlays, the willingness of the owners of mobile devices to provide resources and services to others does not only depend on the technical feasibility. In fact, we conducted a user poll among students and employees of KIT that indicated that—beside security considerations—device owners are mostly concerned about spending their scarce energy resources. This observation is also underlined by a survey, which concludes that energy is the most limiting factor for sharing resources of mobile devices in a grid-like fashion [6].

Motivated by this observation, CoMoGriP develops a framework for provisioning grid services on mobile devices with fine-grained control of the energy consumption. A prototype of this framework has been successfully demonstrated [4]. The framework builds upon OSGi as a tool for distributed service provisioning as shown in Figure 5. New components developed by CoMoGriP include a *local energy manager* keeping track of energy spent for resource sharing, an *energy estimator* that predicts energy consumption of a service call, and different *service selection policies* that enable, e. g., fair energy sharing between all devices or extending the time until first failure of a device or service. Although this enables energy-aware service provisioning, one must keep in mind that energy is not only consumed by the services them self, but also by service management. Energy consumption for management operations can be reduced by combining the transmission of management and service data [5]. Current work aims on providing incentives for resource sharing by an energy-efficient micro-payment scheme as well as on integrating the energy management framework with the SpoVNet architecture.

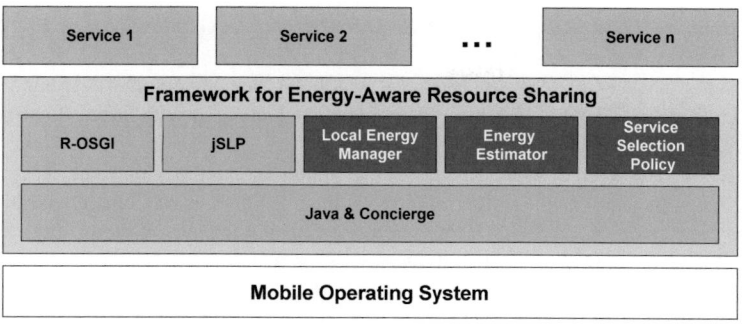

Fig. 5. Architecture of the energy management framework.

Conclusion

Integrating mobile devices in Internet applications imposes new challenges. These hinder the development and deployment of service overlays as a tool to introduce new functionality in the Internet. The young investigator group *Controlling Heterogeneous and Dynamic Mobile Grid and Peer-to-Peer Systems* makes several contributions to cope with this problem, spanning from research results to software tools. It develops a generic architecture for service overlay creation that provides connectivity across heterogeneous networks. Furthermore, it provides mechanisms for boostrapping without infrastructure support. A group communication service is implemented as example for a service overlay. Beyond the context of service overlays, CoMoGriP pays attention to energy as a limiting factor for service provisioning on mobile devices.

References

1. R. Bless, C. Hübsch, S. Mies, and O. Waldhorst. The Underlay Abstraction in the Spontaneous Virtual Networks (SpoVNet) Architecture. In *Proc. 4th EuroNGI Conf. on Next Generation Internet Networks (NGI 2008)*, Krakow, Poland, 2008. *published on CD-ROM.*
2. R. Bless, O. P. Waldhorst, C. P. Mayer, and H. Wippel. Decentralized and Autonomous Bootstrapping for IPv6-based Peer-to-Peer Networks. In *Proc. 2nd German IPv6 Summit*, 2009. *ranked first in IPv6 Contest 2009 by IPv6 Council.*
3. J. Dinger and O. Waldhorst. Decentralized Bootstrapping of P2P Systems: A Practical View. In *Proc. 8th IFIP TC6 Int. Conf. on Networking (Networking 2009)*, pages 703–715, Aachen, Germany, 2009.
4. J. Furthmüller, S. Becker, and O. P. Waldhorst. Demo Abstract: An Energy Manager for a Mobile Grid. In *Proc. 7th ACM Int. Conf. on Mobile Systems, Applications and Services (MobySys 2009)*, Krakow, Poland, 2009.
5. J. Furthmüller, S. Kessler, and O. P. Waldhorst. Energy-efficient Management of Wireless Sensor Networks. In *7th Conf. on Wireless On demand Network Systems and Services (WONS 2010)*, pages 129–136, Kranjska Gora, Slovenia, 2010.
6. J. Furthmüller and O. P. Waldhorst. A Survey on Grid Computing on Mobile Consumer Devices. In N. Antonopoulos, G. Exarchakos, M. Li, , and A. Liotta, editors, *Handbook of*

Research on P2P and Grid Systems for Service-Oriented Computing, pages 313–363. IGI-Global, 2010.

7. C. Hübsch, C. Mayer, S. Mies, R. Bless, O. Waldhorst, and M. Zitterbart. Demo Abstract: Using Legacy Applications in Future Heterogeneous Networks with ariba. In *Proc. IEEE INFOCOM 2010*, San Diego, 2010.

8. C. Hübsch, C. P. Mayer, S. Mies, R. Bless, O. P. Waldhorst, and M. Zitterbart. Reconnecting the Internet with ariba - Self-Organizing Provisioning of End-to-End Connectivity in Heterogeneous Networks. *ACM SIGCOMM Computer Communications Review*, 40(1):131–132, 2010. *SIGCOMM 2009 Best Posters & Demos.*

9. C. Hübsch, C. P. Mayer, and O. P. Waldhorst. On Runtime Adaptation of Application-Layer Multicast Protocol Parameters. In *Proc. IFIP TC6 Conf. on Networked Services and Applications Engineering, Control and Management (EUNICE)*, Trondheim, Norway, June 2010. *to appear.*

10. C. Hübsch, C. P. Mayer, and O. P. Waldhorst. The Ariba Framework for Application Development using Service Overlays. *Praxis der Informationsverarbeitung und Kommunikation (PIK)*, 33(1):7–11, Mar. 2010.

11. C. Hübsch, C. P. Mayer, and O. P. Waldhorst. User-perceived Performance of the NICE Application Layer Multicast Protocol in Large and Highly Dynamic Groups. In *Proc. 15th GI/ITG Int. Conf. on Measurement, Modelling and Evaluation of Computing Systems (MMB 2010)*, pages 62–77, Essen, Germany, 2010. *best paper award.*

12. C. Hübsch and O. P. Waldhorst. Enhancing Application-Layer Multicast Solutions by Wireless Underlay Support. In *Proc. GI/ITG Fachtagung Kommunikation in Verteilten Systemen (KiVS 2009)*, pages 267–272, Kassel, Germany, 2009.

13. E. K. Lua, J. Crowcroft, M. Pias, R. Sharma, and S. Lim. A Survey and Comparison of Peer-to-Peer Overlay Network Schemes. *IEEE Communications Surveys and Tutorials*, 7:72–93, 2005.

14. S. Mies, O. Waldhorst, and H. Wippel. Towards End-to-End Connectivity for Overlays across Heterogeneous Networks. In *Proc. Int. Workshop on the Network of the Future (Future-Net 2009), co-located with IEEE ICC 2009*, Dresden, Germany, 2009. *published on CD-ROM.*

15. O. Waldhorst. On Overlay-based Addressing and Routing in Heterogeneous Future Networks (Invited Paper). In *Proc. 19th Int. IEEE Conf. on Computer Communications and Networks (ICCCN 2010)*, Zürich, Switzerland, Aug. 2010. *to appear.*

16. O. Waldhorst, C. Blankenhorn, D. Haage, R. Holz, G. Koch, B. Koldehofe, F. Lampi, C. Mayer, and S. Mies. Spontaneous Virtual Networks: On the Road towards the Internet's Next Generation. *it — Information Technology (Special Issue on Next Generation Internet)*, 50(6):367–375, 2008.

17. O. Waldhorst, R. Bless, , and M. Zitterbart. Overlay-Netze als Innovationsmotor im Internet. *Informatik-Spektrum*, 33(2):171–185, 2010.

Efficient Usage of Wireless Communication Resources for Safety and non-Safety Vehicular Communication

Natalya An, Jens Mittag, Jérôme Härri

Junior Research Group on Traffic Telematics*
Institute of Telematics
{an,mittag,haerri}@kit.edu

Abstract. Establishing vehicular communication by adding information and communication technologies to vehicles and road infrastructures is a promising approach to improve safety and non-safety related communication for future traffic telematics applications. The objective of the Junior Research Group on Traffic Telematics is to analyze vehicular communication conditions and develop collaborative communication policies between vehicles and with communication infrastructures to provide an efficient and fair usage of the vehicular wireless communication resources.

We first address safety-related communication and propose policies to efficiently share the available channel bandwidth between collaborative WLAN-based communicating vehicles. Our objective is to analyze the conditions creating channel congestions and to provide counter-measures avoiding them. We then also investigate non-safety related communication for which we assume the availability of various alternate communication technologies. We develop an abstract representation of such heterogeneous communication network as a weighted directed graph, where link metrics, such as communication performance or cost, are represented as the graph edges' weights. Such representation would then let traffic applications select or use in a complementary way the best suited communication technologies.

Although less life-critical than safety-related applications, traffic telematics applications based on non-safety related communications, such as distributed traffic density estimation and dynamic traffic re-routing, are nonetheless important as they are expected to ease the market introduction of vehicular communication for traffic telematics. They are also based on a larger scale, both spatially and in the number of actors, and therefore potentially require high computational resources. We therefore finally propose a simulation approach inspired from cloud computing to ease large scale simulation of vehicular communications for future traffic telematics applications.

---

* The Junior Research Group is associated to the Decentralized Systems and Network Services (DSN) Research Group at the Institute of Telematics.

1 Introduction

The field of vehicular communication aims at adding information and communication technologies to transportation infrastructures and vehicles to develop new safety-related traffic telematics applications, such as lane changing warning or collision warning (see Fig. 1), or new non-safety related traffic telematics applications, such as green light optimized speed advisory. By using wireless communication technologies between vehicles and with the road infrastructure, and then interconnect them to form a *Vehicular Network* (also known as a *Vehicular Ad Hoc Network (VANET)*), the required traffic conditions information becomes faster and more precisely available to traffic telematics applications.

As requirements for safety-related traffic telematics applications usually include short transmission delay, dedicated inter-vehicular communication based on the IEEE 802.11 WLAN standard in ad-hoc mode has been preferred, for which a specific 802.11 standard, the IEEE 802.11p, is currently being specified and standardized by the IEEE and adopted also by the European Telecommunication Standards Institute (ETSI)[1] for the ITS-G5 PHY/MAC layer Intelligent Transportation System (ITS) European profile. A 30 Mhz dedicated frequency band at 5.8 GHz has been allocated by the European Commission for safety and non-safety related communications.

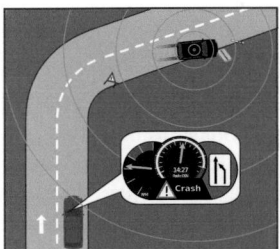

Fig. 1. Safety-related vehicular communication - The blue vehicle is informed via vehicular communication of the upcoming, yet hidden, black car accident.

Due to the limited bandwidth allocated for vehicular communication and the potential high number of communicating vehicles, the wireless channel is expected to become congested. It will in turn lower the communication performance and accordingly challenge the reception of safety-related communication. To mitigate this aspect, congestion control techniques, such as adapting the transmit power or rate, should be developed to efficiently and dynamically share the available bandwidth between communicating vehicles. The CAR 2 CAR Communication Consortium[2], to which the Institute of Telematics at the KIT is

---

[1] A technical committee at the ETSI is in charge of the standardization process of the communication aspects of Intelligent Transportation Systems (ITS). See http://portal.etsi.org/portal/server.pt/community/ITS/317

[2] CAR 2 CAR Communication Consortium (C2CCC). http://www.car-to-car.org/

development member, as well as the ETSI acknowledged this aspect and created dedicated task forces to develop and standardize congestion control methods.

For non-safety related applications, research focus shifts due to different applications demands. For instance, delay tolerance is higher and the destination area is usually much wider than a local neighborhood, potentially even spanning worldwide through the Internet. To this objective, alternate technologies such as cellular technologies (IEEE 802.16, 3G) are envisioned to be jointly employed with 802.11 WLAN. The challenge then becomes to efficiently choose the most efficient communication technology to fulfill the user and/or application requirements. To investigate this, we propose to use graph theory and represent such heterogeneous vehicular communication network as a weighted directed graph, where vehicles and infrastructure nodes are abstracted as graph vertices, while communication links are abstracted as graph edges, which weights are build based on communication performance or cost.

Whereas it is crucial to test and evaluate the impact of vehicular communication on safety and non-safety related applications in real field tests, aspects such as driver safety, logistic difficulties, economic issues and technology limitations make simulation the mean of choice and a widely adopted first step in development of real-world technologies. Considering that simulation-based evaluations of vehicular communication for such applications, notably the non-safety related ones, would require scenarios including a large number of vehicles potentially spread over a large area, e.g. a part or an entire city, high demand in processing power will surely be required. It is therefore also crucial to investigate methodologies to efficiently use available simulation resources.

In order to address the aspects previously described, the Junior Research Group on Traffic Telematics (VTM) has been founded in 2008 and is supported with a leading investigator and two research assistants by the Ministry of Science, Research and the Arts of Baden-Württemberg , the Klaus Tschira Stiftung, the INIT GmbH and the PTV AG. For safety-related communication, the VTM group investigates solutions to control the channel congestion, and designs more efficient cooperative transmit power control techniques, while for non-safety related communication, it studies the properties of heterogeneous vehicular communication networks to follow the concept of "always best connected (ABC)", notably related to vehicular delay tolerant networks. In order to offer a scalable methodology for the simulations of vehicular communications for traffic telematics, the VTM group further adopts the concept introduced by cloud computing of differentiation of the usage of a resource or a service from its physical location on remote computing platforms, and proposes a solution enabling simulations of vehicular communication and traffic telematics application as-a-service.

The remaining of this paper is organized as follows. Section 2 describes the work conducted in improving safety-related vehicular communication, while Section 3 covers heterogeneous vehicular networks for non-safety related communication. In Section 4, we describe our simulation-as-a-service concept, while we provide some long-term potential research directions in Section 5. Section 6 finally summarizes this work.

2 Safety-related Communication

Road safety has been a long-term endeavor for public authorities, automobile industry and researchers worldwide. The rapid evolution of wireless communication technology and its significant cost reduction in recent years have opened a new door to traffic safety through *Vehicular Ad Hoc Networks (VANETs)*. Radio-equipped vehicles are assumed to directly exchange information and, thus, to exceed the boundaries of locally available knowledge (see Fig. 1). Distributed safety applications running in each vehicle are thereby envisioned to assist the driver by making use of the enhanced information set.

From a communication perspective, VANETs have to ensure that the communication traffic generated by the sending vehicles can be served by the wireless medium. For traffic safety it is assumed that each vehicle will proactively send out periodic one-hop messages (called beacons) to establish mutual awareness. In addition, when a hazardous situation is detected, 'reactive' or 'event-driven' emergency messages will be send out. Without controlling the vehicles' communication behavior, one can easily be confronted with stressed and saturated channel conditions simply due to the transmissions of periodic messages (see Fig. 2). Hence, one needs to control the load or the share of the channel imposed by the periodic messages to allow for reliable and low-latency transmissions of high-priority emergency messages.

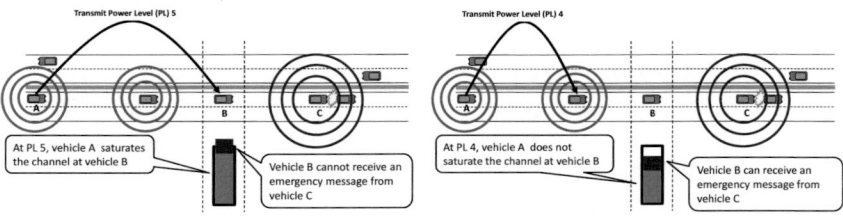

(a) With a high transmit power for beacons, channel is saturated and cannot serve an emergency message

(b) With a reduced transmit power for beacons, channel is available for an emergency message

Fig. 2. Congestion control concept for safety-related vehicular communication.

To avoid saturated and congested channel conditions, we developed in [1] a distributed congestion control protocol called Distributed Fair Power Adjustment for Vehicular Environments (D-FPAV) that reduces the transmission power used for periodic messages such that a maximum (pre-defined) load level on the wireless channel is not exceeded. Since every vehicle is assumed to adjust its transmission power autonomously, the protocol first ensures that each vehicles obtains a sufficient amount of knowledge about the detailed network topology in the surrounding and then uses this information as input for the localized FPAV algorithm that implements a max-min fairness for the final power selection. By providing the same – or at least very similar – information about the surrounding network topology to all vehicles within a certain area, neighboring vehicles compute equal or only slightly different transmission power values.

Admittedly, the provisioning of the algorithm input introduces a vast communication overhead, and is therefore not suitable for a practical deployment. Indeed, an extensive simulation study showed that the overhead can grow up to 40 %. In order to come closer to a practical solution, we performed in [2] an analysis of the requirements for effective and low-overhead transmission power control in VANETs. In particular, we studied the amount of topology information required to effectively control the load on the channel and came to the conclusion that topology knowledge within 2 hops is required. As a result, we modified the provisioning part of the D-FPAV protocol to provide only abstracted or approximated topology information. By exchanging only the average observed vehicle densities (in terms of histograms) instead of individual vehicle positions, we were able reduce the overhead down to 0,42 %. The new protocol also consists explicitly of two parts: the Distributed Vehicle Density Estimation (DVDE) and the Segment-based Power Adjustment for Vehicular environemnts (SPAV) mechanisms.

In [3], we then studied whether one could reduce the load and the congestion on the wireless channel by disseminating periodic beacon messages over multiple hops with event further reduced transmit powers. Due to the relaying over multiple hops, this approach would provide the same dissemination distance as the one-hop approach with higher transmission power, but at the benefit of an increased spatial reuse of the channel. And indeed, as our study revealed, it is possible to further reduce the load, at least in theory where optimal conditions and a perfect behavior of the distributed multi-hop dissemination protocol are observed. However, in distributed environments, this optimality is not achieved, e.g. due to the significant known hidden station problem is significant in a VANET scenario, and the benefit is lost.

In the future, we plan to investigate techniques that promise to solve the hidden station problem in vehicular ad-hoc networks, at least to a sufficient degree. By solving the hidden station problem, we are able to achieve a protocol behavior that is closer to optimality and which can then exploit the benefits that are only observed in theory so far. Since most of the promising techniques are located on the physical layer, we have developed in [4] a detailed physical layer simulator for the IEEE 802.11p standard and integrated it into the popular network simulator NS-3. The resulting simulation framework will be the foundation for the evaluation of such techniques and their impact on the performance of the vehicular network, in particular the impact on the performance and behavior of distributed communication protocols for safety-related communication.

3 Heterogeneous Vehicular Communication

Along with efforts to increase safety on the roads, vehicular communication is investigated to support non-safety related applications, such as green light optimized speed advisory or infotainment. The class of non-safety related applications is broad and varies in such aspects as accepted latency, required bandwidth, intended destination nodes, communication patterns, level of infrastructure involvement and so on. Heterogeneous communication exploits various communication standards and is believed to be a suitable solution to support such applications, as heterogeneous communication itself, exhibits a wide range of technological capabilities and infrastructure features. As most of the non-safety related applications can tolerate various delay when compared to safety related applications we are interested in delay-tolerant applications.

In Heterogeneous Vehicular Networks (HVNs), a vehicle is assumed to be equipped with multiple radio interfaces and capable to make use of various available communication technologies. Communication patterns are thus not limited to dedicated vehicle-to-vehicle communication, but also include communication between vehicles and infrastructure, such as cellular base stations or road-side units. Also delay tolerance of non-safety related applications allows store-carry-and-forward approach as a communication pattern. Although these make ubiquitous networking in HVN possible, additional challenges appear, i.e., choosing between a set of available network access possibilities, and hence, selecting between several communication patterns the best one at a certain point of time and space. The objective is not to substitute one technology by another, or find one that fits all needs, but rather to internetwork available technologies and complement each others for a better performance. For instance, a vehicle having immediate cellular access may opt to wait for a WLAN hotspot, which it knows (from e.g. previous experience) it will encounter later along the way, and which will provide necessary bandwidth for the application for an acceptable monetary cost. Or, when performance is more important and the user is willing to pay more, it may choose to select cellular network immediately. These choices will change depending not only on available technologies or application requirements, but also depending on the time of a day, load in the network or operator's billing policies. We, therefore, investigate the dynamic selection of the appropriate technology to support ubiquitous networking in HVNs based on connectivity costs, network conditions and requirements of the specific applications.

To study the feasibility and to analyze the benefits of such heterogeneous communication we pursue the following approach: We abstract a HVN as a weighted directed graph, where each node, irrespectively, whether it is a vehicle or a part of an infrastructure, is represented as a vertex and where each existing link between two nodes is represented as an edge. The weights are built based on a set of metrics, e.g., link duration, delay, received power, capacity and represent the attractiveness of one link over the others. We do not focus on various wireless communication standards, but rather on their fundamental features, such as on PHY or MAC layers that contribute to the weights of the communication links they support. Fig. 3 illustrates this approach, with the HVN on the left and its graph abstraction on the right. In the graph, one could see the abstraction of vehicles and infrastructure as nodes, and connectivity links with edges. Quality of the links is determined by the weight function that each link possesses.

Our current research focuses on the study of relevant metrics to build such weight function, along with their meaningful representation. We investigate if knowledge of the relevant metrics and weights may give a realistic insight on

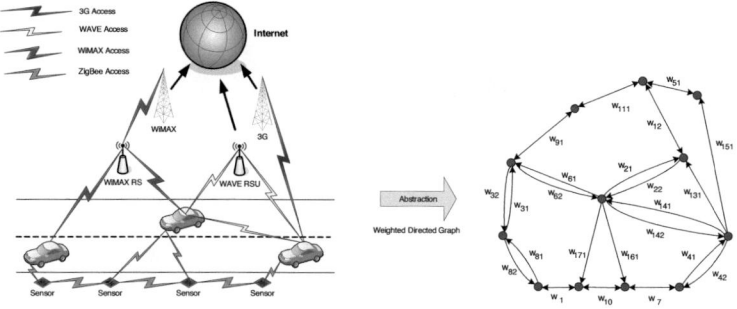

Fig. 3. Abstraction of Heterogeneous Vehicular Network as a weighted directed graph.

expected network performance. As well as whether they can be used to optimize network and transport protocols along with infrastructure placement and usage.

4 Simulating Traffic Telematics Applications as a Service

The development of vehicular communication requires the evaluation of their impacts on network-wide communication protocols, on which safety and non-safety related traffic telematics could be based. For logistics, flexibility, and financial reasons, evaluations using simulations are usually preferred over field tests, as they offer a large modularity in the evaluated communication protocols and full flexibility in the chosen scenarios. Considering the large scale typically involved in traffic telematics scenarios, simulations also require high computational capabilities including maintenance and technical expertise potentially resulting in significant financial investments on local simulation infrastructures. Moreover, such infrastructures are usually not efficiently used, in a sense that they are overused when simulations are conducted and underused when not.

Cloud computing is a novel paradigm that offers a differentiation of the usage of a resource or a service and its physical location on remote High Capacity Computing (HCC) platforms. Typical benefits from this approach are for instance an improved resource sharing between remote users, user-friendly web-based access to and configuration of a service, efficient maintenance and easier extensibility. Based on this concept, we proposed in [5] a *Simulation-as-a-Service* approach to evaluate vehicular communication and traffic telematics applications. We segment a simulation process into two building blocks: a *Web-interface/server Front-end* to configure the remote simulations, and a *Back-end* consisting of a controller and a HCC platform to conduct the remote simulations (see Fig. 4). Our objective is to illustrate how simulations requiring a large number of executions could be configured on a web-interface and remotely run in parallel on HCC platforms, for example on the High Performance Computing (HPC) platform of the Steinbuch Center for Computing (SCC) [6] at the KIT.

The objective of the *Front-end* is to provide a user-friendly web-based configuration of the simulation study, as well as an interface between the user and the simulation infrastructure. A web-interface gathers the inputs from users regardless of their location or used device, while the web-server saves the scenarios

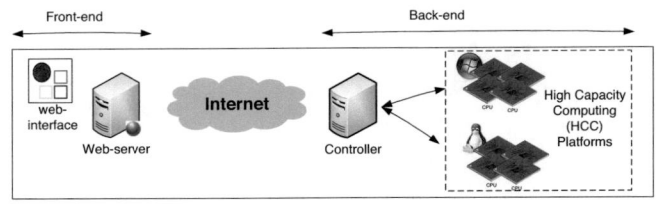

Fig. 4. Simulation-as-a-Service - Front-end and Back-end Concepts as proposed in [5].

and other data transmitted by the users, connects to the back-end, transmits the simulation scenarios to the controller and retrieves and stores the simulation results. The front-end technology is based on the Eclipse framework and on the Eclipse Rich Ajax Platform (RAP) [7]. It has been chosen as it allows the development of AJAX-enabled applications based on the Eclipse Rich Client Platform (RCP) as well as for its convenient user-interfaces.

The *Back-end* consists of a *Controller* connected to a HCC platform. The controller is in charge of configuring the HCC platform as well as distributing and scheduling the simulations on it. As for HCC, we use the HPC of the SCC [6], which provides us with a computing capability of approx. 800 GFLOPS on average. The back-end also employs Kernel-based Virtual Machines (KVM) [8], a hardware virtualization solution for Linux on recent x86 and x86-64 processors. This approach let us run fully configurable Windows or Linux images adapted to the simulation requirements on the HCC platforms and allows us to benefit from high computation capacities regardless of the simulation environment.

In the future, we would like to extend the concept to add modularity in the simulation environment. A solution currently followed is the design of a middleware following the concepts of *High Layer Architecture (HLA) [9]* located in the back-end. As a function of the required level of details provided by the user in the front-end for safety or non safety-related communication, such a middleware would couple appropriate models such as transceiver, communication protocol, and vehicular mobility. Another approach followed is to provide identity management solutions allowing administrators to provide a personal space for users and to control their access rights to simulation resources.

5   Long Term Vision

We focused so far mainly in the analysis and improvements of vehicular communication, as this is a complex and challenging domain which, as a corner stone to improve traffic telematics applications, should be carefully investigated. Yet, in the future, and considering heterogeneous communication technologies, we expect that the challenges of traffic telematics applications be shifted from a vehicular communication perspective to a vehicular system and service perspective, where communication will be assumed and the objective will be to interconnect different systems, operator, or users to provide services to customers. For example, the Internet Multimedia Subsystem (IMS) could be envisioned to also include vehicular communication for instance, or considering heterogeneous operators and services, identity management for traffic telematics applications is expected to also attract attentions in the future.

Vehicular communication should also not be limited to cars, but should also include any kind of public or private transportation system. For instances, the safety and non-safety related aspects may easily be imagined also for communicating between trams, trains and cars. Considering safety-related communications, the Karlsuhe Transport Agency (KVV) recently suffered from two important accidents involving trams and cars. Would trams or cars be made aware of their mutual movements early enough, would such accident probably be avoided. For non-safety related communication, another promising traffic telematics application considering such generalized vehicular communication environment could be multi-modal transportation, where communication between vehicles and road infrastructures is used to improve the collaboration between public and private transportation, typically for traffic planning, with the objective to further convince commuters and travelers to rely more on public transportation instead of solely using the private counterpart.

If such effort succeeds, commuting could be seen from a different perspective, as travelers would get liberated from the stress of driving and thus could use this time either for their spare time, or to be connected to their workplace. The former aspect would add comfort to daily commuting, while the latter would shift the potentially time loss to productive work time spent in a virtual desk in public transportation. Accordingly, it becomes crucial for public transportation operators to provide a wide range of services to the on-board travelers adapted to their cost-performance expectations.

6 Summary

Believing that vehicular communication will have a crucial role in improving existing traffic telematics application or even be the key for the creation of novel ones, the Junior Research Group on Traffic Telematics focused on investigating the challenges and improving the usage of vehicular wireless communication resources. We designed methods to efficiently share the available vehicular communication channel between users for safety-related communication, and also proposed and investigated a graph-based representation of heterogeneous vehicular networks based on various communication technologies to optimize the network access for non-safety related communication. We finally designed a simulation-as-a-service approach to evaluate the benefits of our improved vehicular communication solutions, typically for large-scale traffic telematics scenarios.

Following the motivating results illustrated in this paper, we further believe that more exciting developments in the previously described research domains, as well as in the identified future directions, are yet to be discovered and evaluated. Our hope and conviction is that one day, vehicles will be able to effectively talk each others to extend the horizon of awareness of drivers and avoid accidents, to reduce traffic congestion and the related high carbon footprint, as well as to allow vehicles to be fully part and actors of the Internet.

Acknowledgments

Natalya An, Jens Mittag and Jérôme Härri would like to thank the Ministry of Science, Research and the Arts of Baden-Württemberg (Az: Zu 33-827.377/19,20), the Klaus Tschira Stiftung, the INIT GmbH and the PTV AG for their support to the Junior Research Group on Traffic Telematics.

We would also like to thank Prof. Dr. Martina Zitterbart for having initiated this Junior Research Group, Prof. Dr. Hannes Hartenstein for his help and guidance, as well as all members of his *Decentralized Systems and Network Services (DSN)* Research Group for their fruitful discussions and collaborations.

Further Information related to the Junior Research Group may be found on the group's website at: `http://dsn.tm.kit.edu/english/nvt.php`

References

1. Torrent-Moreno, M., Mittag, J., Santi, P., Hartenstein, H.: Vehicle-to-Vehicle Communication: Fair Transmit Power Control for Safety-Critical Information. IEEE Transactions on Vehicular Technology, Volume 58, Issue 7, pp. 3684-3707, Sept. 2009.
2. Mittag, J., Schmidt-Eisenlohr, F., Killat, M., Härri, J., Hartenstein, H.: Analysis and Design of Effective and Low-Overhead Transmission Power Control for VANETs. Proc. of the 5th ACM International Workshop on Vehicular Ad Hoc Networks (VANET), pp. 39-48, San Francisco, California, USA, Sept. 2008.
3. Mittag, J., Thomas, F., Härri, J., Hartenstein, H.: A Comparison of Single- and Multi-hop Beaconing in VANETs. Proc. of the 6th ACM International Workshop on Vehicular Ad Hoc Networking (VANET), pp. 69-78, Bejing, China, Sept. 2009.
4. Papanastasiou, S., Mittag, J., Ström, E.G., Hartenstein, H.: Bridging the Gap between Physical Layer Emulation and Network Simulation. Proc. of the IEEE Wireless Communications and Networking Conference, Sydney, Autralia, Apr. 2010.
5. Härri, J. , Killat, M., Tielert, T., Mittag, J., Hartenstein, H.: Simulation-as-a-Service for ITS Applications. Proc. of the 3rd IEEE International Symposium on Wireless Vehicular Communications (WiVeC), Taipei, Taiwan, May 2010.
6. Steinbuch Center for Computing at the KIT, `http://scc.kit.edu`
7. The Eclipse Rich Ajax Platform (RAP), `http://www.eclipse.org/rap/`
8. Kernel-based Virtual Machine, `http://www.linux-kvm.org/`
9. IEEE Standard for Modeling and Simulation (M&S) High Level Architecture (HLA) Framework and Rules, IEEE Std 1516-2000, IEEE, 2000.

Biography

Natalya An holds a Master of Science (M.Sc.) degree in Communications Engineering from RWTH Aachen University, Germany. She is a research assistant and a Ph.D. student within the junior research group on Traffic Telematics at the Institute of Telematics. Her research interests include vehicular ad hoc networks and heterogeneous vehicular networks.

Jens Mittag holds a diploma (Dipl.-Inform.) in Computer Science from the University of Karlsruhe, Germany. He is a research assistant and a Ph.D. student within the junior research group on Traffic Telematics at the Institute of Telematics. His research interests include mobile networks, simulation environments and, more recently, the modeling of wireless lower physical layers.

Jérôme Härri is an assistant professor and leading investigator of the junior research group on Traffic Telematics at the Institute of Telematics. His research interests include inter-vehicular communication, vehicular mobility modeling and management and delay critical or tolerant networks. He holds a diploma and a doctoral degree (Dr. ès Sc.) in Telecommunication from the Swiss Institute Technology (EPFL), Switzerland.

Designing Energy-Efficient, Predictable, and Reliable Real-Time and Embedded Systems

Jian-Jia Chen

Chair of Micro Hardware Technologies for Automation
Institut für Prozessrechentechnik, Automation und Robotik (IPR)
Department of Informatics
Karlsruhe Institute of Technology (KIT), Karlsruhe, Germany
email:jian-jia.chen@kit.edu

Abstract. Embedded systems have been widely adopted and deployed in many application domains, while the average or worst-case response time in many applications is a non-functional but important requirement. For best-effort systems, such as telecommunication devices or hand-held applications, the average response time is expected to be short to maintain the good reactivity and good dependability. For critical-control systems, such as automotive controllers or automated aircraft landing systems, high reactivity and high dependability must be ensured by the worst-case response time guarantee to maintain the safety and the stability of the systems. There are many challenges for designing embedded systems, to satisfy functional properties, such as compilers, embedded programming languages, etc., and non-functional properties, such as energy reduction, reliability, timing predictability, etc. The chair of Micro Hardware Technologies for Automation focuses on the design and analysis of the non-functional properties for real-time embedded systems. This article presents current research and future research directions, in the chair, for designing energy-efficient, predictable, and reliable real-time and embedded systems.

1 Introduction

Embedded systems have been widely adopted in many domains, such as telecommunication devices, smart-phone applications, automotive controllers, and navigation systems. To ensure the stability, dependability, and safety, in additional to the functional properties, an embedded system has to satisfy non-functional properties, such as timing satisfaction, energy reduction, reliability assurance. The Chair of Micro Hardware Technologies for Automation focuses on the design and analysis of real-time and embedded systems, specifically, for the following topics: (1) Low-Power and Energy-Efficient Considerations, (2) Energy-Constrained Systems, (3) Timing Predictability of MPSoCs (multiprocessor systems on chip), and (4) Reliability Issues.

Low-Power and Energy-Efficient Considerations Performance boosting has been a highly important goal in system designs in the past decades. Not until recently, energy efficiency becomes another critical feature being pursued in a wide variety of products, especially for battery-driven embedded devices. How to achieve the balance between the system performance and the power consumption triggers the advance of the dynamic voltage scaling (DVS) technology, which provides a means to adjust the supply voltage and thus the speed of microprocessors. Energy-efficient scheduling has been an active research topic in both industry and academics. As higher power density in modern circuits also leads to higher temperature, heat is another issue that must be considered for system designs. Even though both heat generation and energy consumption are related to power dissipation, temperature and energy are physical entities with different properties. The minimization of energy consumption is to prolong the lifetime of the battery or to cut down the power bills. The minimization of the peak temperature can help reduce the packing cost or to prevent the processor from over-heating.

Energy-Constrained Systems The emerging technology of energy harvesting has earned much interest recently to provide a means for sustainable embedded systems. For systems with expensive deployment cost, energy harvested from the environment could provide sustainable services. Among renewable energy resources, energy harvesting with solar panels is one of the most popular applied technologies, and there have been many energy harvesting circuits that are designed to efficiently convert and store solar energy. Clearly, one may just use solar energy to recharge a primary energy source, e.g. a battery. In this way, the point in time when the system runs out of energy is simply postponed. If, however, one strives for perpetual operation, common power management techniques have to be reconceived. Then the embedded system has to adapt to the stochastic nature of the solar energy. Goal of this adaptation is to maximize the utility of the application in a long-term perspective. The resulting mode of operation is sometimes also called energy neutral operation: The performance of the application is not predetermined a priori, but adjusted in a best effort manner during runtime and ultimately dictated by the power source. To use the energy/power effectively, decisions like when to provide which service have to be made in order to satisfy the needs of the user as well as possible. Two major constraints arise due to the common energy sources: (1) The harvested energy is temporarily low and the services must be lowered or suspended. (2) During bursts, the harvested energy exceeds the battery capacity.

Timing Predictability of MPSoCs In modern embedded systems with off-the-shelf (COTS) components, multiprocessor systems on chip (MPSoCs) and multicore platforms have been applied. For such systems, shared resources, such as memory or I/O peripherals for communication and data exchange between cores, are deployed. However, multiple processing elements competing for access to a shared resource yields contention and as a result, significantly increased worst-case response time. Accesses to the shared resources increase the worst-case response time of a task, and decrease the predictability of the system.

Reliability Issues Traditionally, reliability and fault tolerance concerns are mainly the task left for hardware manufacturing in computer system designs. However, as VLSI design has come to the nano age, components, circuits, and devices are prone to un-reliability. Designing solutions to resolve these reliability issues is a task that must be considered in both hardware and software levels. A fault of an unreliable component results in two consequences: either permanent or temporal failure of the component. The former fault is called hard (permanent) fault, while the latter is referred to as soft (transient) fault. For digital systems at the nano age, these faults have become more significant. For instance, aging mechanisms such as electromigration (EM) or negative bias temperature instability (NBTI) would lead to hard faults, and the component is not reliable or functional anymore. In contrast, the cosmic ray radiations result in soft faults, in which the computation or stored result of a component could be only temporally in-correct. Hard (permanent) faults are not recoverable, and, hence, have to be considered carefully during the system design phase to prevent the system from early failure. Soft (transient) faults can be recovered from incorrect states with re-computation or apply-ing error-correction code. Therefore, in the nano age, we have to consider unreliability while designing dependable systems, in particular embedded systems. Design and anal-ysis of the reliability of a real-time embedded system with unreliable (sub-)components would help system designers understand whether the system is dependable.

2 Current Research

2.1 Low-Power and Energy-Efficient Considerations

For a CMOS processor, the power consumption mainly comes from two parts: (1) the dynamic power mainly resulting from the charging and dis-charging of CMOS gates and (2) the static power mainly resulting from the leakage current. For technologies in micrometer scales, the dynamic power dominates the power consumption, while the two sources are comparable for nano-meter technologies. A system is slowed down to reduce the energy consumption from the dynamic power, and is turned off (or to some dormant modes) to reduce that from the static power. The research focuses of the chair in low-power and energy-efficient designs are on (1) uniprocessor systems, for example, [2,3,10], (2) homogeneous multiprocessor systems, for example, [1], and (3) heterogeneous multiprocessor systems, for example, [4,7].

Heat is an issue that must be considered for system designs to prevent from failure or to improve the reliability. We have proposed analysis and algorithms for (a) peak temperature minimization in real-time systems [8] and (b) schedulability tests for real-time tasks under the peak temperature constraint [5].

2.2 Energy-Constrained Systems

While most conventional power management solutions aim to save energy subject to given performance constraints, performance constraints might not be given a priori for the energy harvesting systems. Rather, the performance is adapted in a best effort man-ner according to the availability of environmental energy. The goal is to optimize the performance of the application subject to given energy constraints. In particular, in [11], we provide a set of algorithms and methods for different application scenarios, includ-ing real-time scheduling, application rate control as well as service level allocation.

The purpose of the latter two approaches is to decide which and how many tasks are executed in a long-term perspective. Based on an estimation of the energy harvested in the future, long-term decisions on the use of the available energy are made. On a task level, we provide real-time scheduling algorithms to assign energy to upcoming tasks in a short-term perspective. By taking into account both available time and energy, an optimal task ordering is computed to avoid deadline violations.

2.3 Timing Predictability of MPSoCs

For multiprocessor platforms, tasks that execute on different processing elements require communication among each other and to shared memory to fetch data and instructions. Contention on shared resources, and on shared memory in particular, significantly increases the worst-case response time of tasks. The time-division multiple access (TDMA) protocol for resource arbitration has been adopted in industrial applications to increase timing predictability and to simplify timing analysis. For simplicity, we assume a given task partition is assigned to execute on a processing element. The most related work is by Rosen et al. [12] for analyzing the worst-case behavior of task execution based on the execution traces that are derived from static analysis of a program. Contrary to that, we assume that the positions of accesses to the shared resource are not known a priori and neither is their order.

To characterize the dynamic resource access behavior, we use a superblock model. Superblocks may contain branches and loops, but superblocks themselves are executed sequentially. The execution of superblocks on a processing element is either
(i) sequential, i.e., a succeeding superblock is activated as soon as its preceding superblock has finished, or
(ii) time-triggered, i.e., a superblock starts execution at a predefined time.

Superblocks are specified by their maximum computation time and their maximum number of access requests to a shared resource. A TDMA scheduling policy is applied to grant access to the shared resource. In [14], we explore the worst-case response time analysis for different models to access shared resources within superblocks. In the *dedicated* model, resources are accessed in *acquisition* (**A**) and *replication* (**R**) phases at the beginning and the end of each superblock, respectively. An *execution* (**E**) phase in between issues no access requests to shared resources. The *general* model allows to access a shared resource at any time during a superblock's active time, i.e., the acquisition and replication phases merge with the execution phase. In the *hybrid* model an acquisition and an replication phase exist, but accesses to shared resource can also happen during the execution phase.

We can derive several access models from these definitions:
DS – dedicated sequential phases, sequential superblocks. Superblocks execute sequentially, and accesses to the shared resource are in the acquisition and replication phases. In this model, the emphasis lies on the separation of accesses to the shared resource and computations.
GS – General sequential phases, sequential superblocks.
HS – Hybrid sequential phases, sequential superblocks.
GTS – general sequential phases, time triggered superblocks.

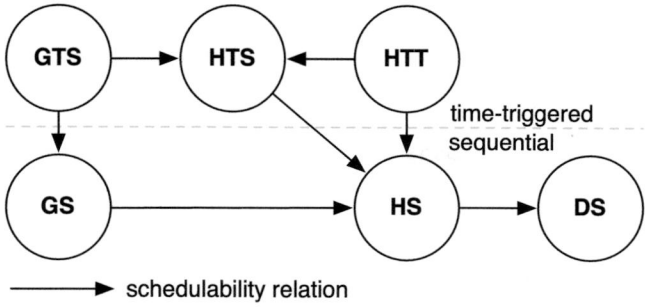

Fig. 1. Schedulability Relationship between different models.

HTS – hybrid sequential phases, time triggered superblocks.
HTT – hybrid time triggered phases, time triggered superblocks.

In [13], a hierarchy of schedulability relations among these six models can be derived. A system is said schedulable if all the tasks can meet their timing constraints. In contrast to intuition, which would dictate that an all time triggered model (**HTT**) would perform best and deliver the best result in terms of predictability, we show that **DS** is most suitable for predictability and efficiency: If any of the six models results as schedulable, the *sequential dedicated model (DS)* is schedulable as well. Therefore, the separation of accesses to the shared resource from computation according to **DS** is the model of choice for multiprocessor resource-sharing systems. Therefore, the sequential dedicated model is the model of choice for multiprocessor, resource sharing systems.

2.4 Reliability Issues

There have been several hardware and software fault detection techniques proposed in the recent years. Traditionally, one can use N-modular redundancy to determine the correct results by voting. However, as hardware redundancy requires additional area and power, the concurrent error detection (CED) technique is more acceptable by combining hardware-level and software-level cooperation. If a single bit error is detected in an ECC protection path in the hardware, there are methods, such as instruction retry, applicable to re-execute the protected path from a saved checkpoint. Redundant multi-threading can also help improve the reliability to resolve the transient faults. Moreover, to determine the lifetime or the mean-time-to-failure (MTTF) of a system in the early stage, the designers have to analyze the reliability issues resulting from the hard faults, especially related to the aging mechanisms.

To resolve soft faults in real-time systems, one might integrate fault tolerance techniques and task scheduling. Moreover, as transient fault rates increase at lower supply voltages [16], one can trade the energy consumption for reliability by applying DVSR. To tolerate the hard and soft faults, task replication has been applied on redundant hardwares. For example, Gopalakrishnan and Caccamo [9] explored the minimization problem of the maximum utilization of processors with a *constant* number of heterogeneous multiprocessors. To cope with the reliability issues in embedded systems, we have already explored task mapping algorithms in [6] to schedule real-time tasks with replications in identical multiprocessor systems and scheduling algorithms in [17] to provide reliability-aware energy management for real-time tasks with probabilistic execution times.

3   Future Research Directions

The focus of the future research direction of the chair is to continue to explore how to design energy-efficient, predictable, and reliable real-time and embedded systems for modern hardware platforms, software technologies, and general event models.

Power-Aware Computing   It is expected that low-power and energy-efficient issues will still play important roles for designing computing systems. In addition to periodic and sporadic real-time applications in the current research focus, the chair is going to consider real-time systems characterized by event streams, in which the arrival of real-time tasks is modeled by arrival curves in the interval domain [15]. Based on the model of event streams, one can predict, in worst cases and best cases, how many events will arrive in the near future, and, hence, the scheduler has to adjust the execution speed or to change the system mode for energy consumption minimization without violating the timing constraints. Based on the general models, the chair is also interested in system-wide energy optimization, including impacts on I/O peripheral, memory control, dynamic power management, dynamic voltage scaling, etc. Of course, how to distribute event streams and events to minimize the energy consumption and how to synthesize platforms for timing satisfaction and energy minimization are also considered as future research directions.

Energy-Harvesting Wireless Sensor Networks   Even though energy management for WSN has been widely explored in the literature to reduce the energy consumption for packet routing, wireless sensor networks with energy-harvesting components require a paradigm shift in the design of routing algorithms, media access protocol (MAC) adaption, and power management. For battery-operated networks, one might distribute the workload as uniform as possible to maximize lifetime under given workload. For energy-harvesting networks, the environmental power should be exploited effectively and efficiently to maximize the workload under environmental constraints. The chair is going to look for designing adaptive methods to react to the dynamic behavior of energy harvesting wireless sensor networks, including dynamic routing algorithms, adaptive MACs, etc.

Timing Predictability for Resource Interaction and Contention   Deriving the worst-case response time is not trivial when there are shared resources and tasks have to compete for the shared resources. As the preliminary studies have been done for simple arbiters of shared resources in [13, 14], the chair would like to consider how to design and analyze more general and more efficient models. For example, one could combine dynamic and static arbiters for a shared resource, such as the FlexRay protocol in automotive applications. This would isolate the resource access to ensure the progress and also improve the performance when the other tasks do not access the shared resource. Another line of future research direction is to exploit resource reservation servers, such as Constant Bandwidth Server (CBS) and Total Bandwidth Server (TBS), to isolate the resource accesses. The focus will be (1) to analyze the timing predictability based on given arbiters and resource access models, and (2) to design the arbiters to trade the predictability and efficiency, and (3) to advance the hardware/software technologies to achieve predictable embedded platforms.

Reliability for Real-Time Embedded Systems For designing reliable real-time embedded systems, the chair is going to look for design methods for ensuring the timing properties under designers' reliability, quality of service (QoS), and energy consumption requirements by considering hard faults with hardware redundancy and soft faults with in-time recovery or task replication. For example, to maintain the feasibility of real-time embedded systems, the system has to be reliable in both timing behavior and functionality. If an unreliable component is adopted to build a fully reliable system, one cannot provide feasibility guarantees of the system, as the system could have consecutive faults even with very low probability. For designing a fully reliable system, one possibility is to build hardened circuits, that are designed carefully and pessimistically to avoid faults, and the stringent timing guarantee and the minimal functionality guarantee can be provided by applying the hardened components. Therefore, by adopting hardened components/processors, for hard real-time systems, we would like to maintain the timing guarantees even in the worst cases. That is, the unreliable components can be treated as (a) accelerators, (b) low-power execution units with faults, or (c) helpers to increase the quality of services. Specifically, we would like to investigate, define, and develop concepts to adopt unreliable components and hardened components to understand how to design a reliable system.

Moreover, to cope with soft faults, we would like to explore the reliability guarantee that the system can ensure under timing constraints and the cost optimization under timing and reliability constraints. For multicore/multiprocessor platforms, the mapping of applications and scheduling of tasks should reflect the reliability. Specifically, to deal with hard faults, we would like to investigate how a system should be designed to tolerate multiple hardware failure to extend the lifetime. For soft faults, we would like to explore how to maintain the reliability and timing guarantee with performance optimization to maximize the quality of services or minimize the energy consumption.

4 Long-Term Vision

Embedded systems require several non-functional properties to ensure the dependability, stability, and reactivity. However, modern architectures have imposed many challenges for designing embedded systems. Specifically, the high power density has imposed the energy-efficient and low-power requirements in both hardware and software levels, the shared resources have introduced unpredictable interferences among processing elements, and the hardware faults have addressed the reliability issues. There are still many unsolved problems for designing energy-efficient, predictable, and reliable real-time and embedded systems. The chair hopes to contribute to the fundamental theories and practical studies in this direction.

References

1. Jian-Jia Chen, Heng-Ruey Hsu, and Tei-Wei Kuo. Leakage-aware energy-efficient scheduling of real-time tasks in multiprocessor systems. In *RTAS*, 2006.
2. Jian-Jia Chen and Tei-Wei Kuo. Procrastination for leakage-aware rate-monotonic scheduling on a dynamic voltage scaling processor. In *LCTES*, 2006.
3. Jian-Jia Chen and Tei-Wei Kuo. Procrastination determination for periodic real-time tasks in leakage-aware dynamic voltage scaling systems. In *ICCAD*, pages 289–294, 2007.
4. Jian-Jia Chen and Lothar Thiele. Task partitioning and platform synthesis for energy efficiency. In *RTCSA*, pages 393–402, 2009.
5. Jian-Jia Chen, Shengquan Wang, and Lothar Thiele. Proactive speed scheduling for frame-based real-time tasks under thermal constraints. In *RTAS*, 2009.
6. Jian-Jia Chen, Chuan-Yue Yang, Tei-Wei Kuo, and Shau-Yin Tseng. Real-time task replication for fault tolerance in identical multiprocessor systems. In *RTAS*, pages 249–258, 2007.
7. Edward T.-H. Chu, Tai-Yi Huang, Cheng-Han Tsai, Jian-Jia Chen, and Tei-Wei Kuo. A dvs-assisted hard real-time i/o device scheduling algorithm. *Real-Time Systems*, 41(3):222–255, 2009.
8. Nathan Fisher, Jian-Jia Chen, Shengquan Wang, and Lothar Thiele. Thermal-aware global real-time scheduling on multicore systems. In *RTAS*, pages 131–140, 2009.
9. Sathish Gopalakrishnan and M. Caccamo. Task partitioning with replication upon heterogeneous multiprocessor systems. In *RTAS*, 2006.
10. Kai Huang, Luca Santinelli, Jian-Jia Chen, Lothar Thiele, and Giorgio C. Buttazzio. Adaptive dynamic power management for hard real-time systems. In *RTSS*, pages 23–32, 2009.
11. Clemens Moser, Jian-Jia Chen, and Lothar Thiele. An energy management framework for energy harvesting embedded systems. *ACM Journal on Emerging Technologies in Computing Systems (JETC)*, 2010.
12. J. Rosen, A. Andrei, P. Eles, and Z. Peng. Bus access optimization for predictable implementation of real-time applications on multiprocessor systems-on-chip. In *RTSS*, pages 49–60, 2007.
13. A. Schranzhofer, J.-J. Chen, R. Pellizzoni, L. Thiele, and M. Caccamo. Worst-case response time analysis of resource access models in multi-core systems. In *DAC*, 2010.
14. A. Schranzhofer, J.-J. Chen, and L. Thiele. Timing analysis for TDMA arbitration in resource sharing systems. In *RTAS*, 2010.
15. L. Thiele, S. Chakraborty, and M. Naedele. Real-time calculus for scheduling hard real-time systems. *ISCAS*, 2000.
16. D. Zhu, R. Melhem, and D. Mossé. The effects of energy management on reliability in real-time embedded systems. In *ICCAD*, 2004.
17. Dakai Zhu, Hakan Aydin, and Jian-Jia Chen. Optimistic reliability aware energy management for real-time tasks with probabilistic execution times. In *IEEE Real-Time Systems Symposium*, pages 313–322, 2008.

Software Engineering in the Era of Parallelism

Victor Pankratius

Multicore Software Engineering Young Investigator Group
Karlsruhe Institute of Technology, 76131 Karlsruhe, Germany
pankratius@ipd.uka.de
http://www.victorpankratius.com

Abstract. We are in the era of parallelism: Multicore processors with several cores on the same chip are standard. Fundamental changes in mainstream software development are required, because parallelism is now the key to better performance on every PC, laptop, or embedded device. Every performance-critical application – not just supercomputing applications – has to be parallel in order to exploit the hardware potential. The great challenge is now how to make parallel programming easier for average programmers. This paper presents an overview of my research directions, thoughts, and visions for the field of multicore software engineering, to make parallelism accessible to a large number of developers, scalable, portable, and applicable in novel scenarios. In particular, I will highlight contributions to auto-tuning, programming models, debugging techniques, as well as insights from empirical studies, working towards the goal of making parallel programming easier.

1 Parallelism Changes the Game

The computer science community agrees that we are at an inflection point [1]: Parallelism is available on every desktop at low cost. Every PC, laptop, or embedded device is a truly parallel machine. Regular processors have 4, 8, or 12 cores. Intel presented the Single Chip Cloud Computer prototype with 48 cores on one chip; CISCO had already in 2005 a packet processing chip with 192 cores. Recent graphics cards have over 300 cores that can be used on every PC to speed up data parallel computations. Looking at these developments, it is not hard to believe projections that mainstream processors will soon have hundreds of cores on one chip. We need to take advantage of this horsepower!

In the past, parallel computers used to be expensive and typically accessible to scientists only. Why are they are now affordable for everyone? Processor clock rate increases have reached technical limits, mainly due to heat and power consumption, as shown in Figure 1 (a). We have to go parallel in hardware to increase performance; this is possible because the number of transistors on the same chip can still grow.

What is different from parallel computing in the past? It's not only the ubiquity of parallel hardware, but also some other subtle improvements. Multicore processors share cores as well as other resources, such as cache memory and busses, all on on the same chip (see Figure 1 (b)). This difference has important implications for communication and other overhead, ultimately influencing when parallelization pays off. We are given a new chance in which the break-even sweet spot of parallel performance is moved to a potentially more favorable location, and parallelism becomes applicable in scenarios and fields in everyday life that were never considered before. In addition, we also have new opportunities to exploit parallelism in-the-small, e.g., on a PC or in the pocket cell phone, not just in large-scale distributed systems or supercomputer clusters.

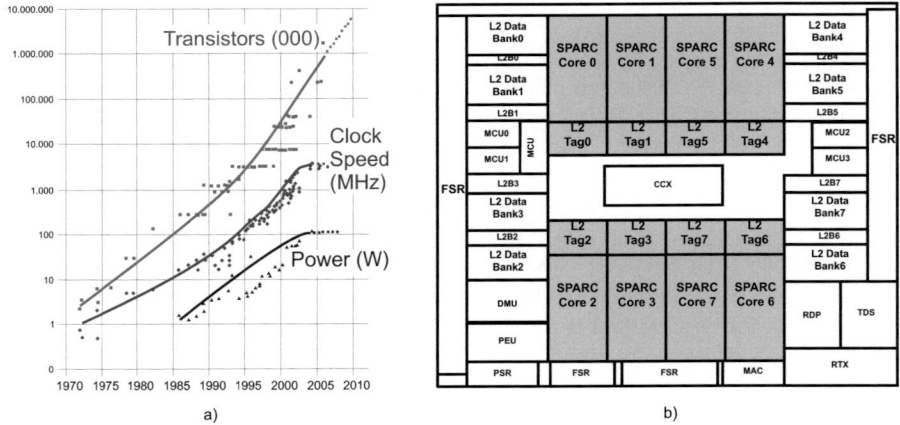

a)   b)

Fig. 1. a) Hardware developments [14]; (b) Sketch of the Sun Niagara II chip [10].

2 Why We Can't Ignore the Trend

Major software engineering methods and tools currently focus on sequential software development. However, every developer is now confronted with parallel programming of applications such as server applications, desktop applications (e.g., compression programs, multimedia programs, games, Web browsers), office applications, or business applications. In addition, parallelism can be used to improve application-level fault-tolerance and human-computer interaction.

Software engineers can't ignore the trend for several reasons. If a particular application is not parallel, it uses just one core, so performance cannot be improved by additional cores. As more and more cores are integrated on the same chip, clock rates may decrease, so if no other techniques are employed sequential applications could be slower on every new processor generation! Needless to say, customers won't buy new systems that have a lower performance than their old ones. Industry projects that all major processor product lines will increase the number of cores in the future. Exploiting parallelism in software becomes an unavoidable necessity.

The whole spectrum of software engineering – from design over testing to maintenance – has to be revisited in the light of parallelism. Nondeterminism adds a new dimension of complexity.

Compared to scientific applications (which I view as the traditional area of parallelism), everyday parallel applications emphasize different requirements. This working hypothesis is grounded on various studies I did in collaboration with industry (e.g., Intel, SAP, and Agilent). For example, exploiting the last few percent of available hardware performance is not so important, while scalability with the number of cores and portability to other platforms is really necessary. Performance can thus be sacrificed in exchange for gaining code that is easier to write, understand, debug, and maintain by teams of developers. Robustness of parallel programs plays a greater role in business-critical or safety-critical systems; scientific simulations can be restarted if something goes wrong, but incorrect financial transactions or flawed security systems may cause irreversible damage in real life. Nevertheless, the trustworthiness of scientific software results would also benefit from better software engineering.

Many parts of the existing software stack require revisions, each providing challenges and opportunities for parallelism exploitation. These parts include programming languages and compilers, libraries, middleware, and operating systems. Although my focus is on the upper layers, all parts are interdependent and have to be adapted and optimized in concert. Software engineering research cannot be looked at in isolation at a higher abstraction level, because the methods and approaches to be developed often rely on certain guarantees enforced in some lower levels. Coping with this interdependency is yet another challenge.

3   Addressing the Multicore Software Engineering Challenge

In the long run, my research aims to make the development of parallel software easier for the average developer by advancing concepts, methods, and tools. My work currently focuses on shared-memory multicore machines. Based on results from empirical studies that will be discussed later, I hypothesize that fully "automagic" parallelization of large, real-world applications is not generally promising. Software engineers need to be involved – more or less directly – in the parallelization process. Automation and tools are meant to support software engineers, assuming they know what to do.

My research takes place in the major areas depicted in Figure 2, which I consider key areas in addressing the difficulties of parallel programming: Automatic performance tuning, parallel programming models, and debugging techniques for parallelism. In addition, empirical studies are an important cross-cutting area serving two purposes: (1) learning about the key issues for each area, based on parallelizing complex real-world applications (most of them in collaboration with industry) as well as studies with programmers; (2) validating new approaches and theories proposed in each research area.

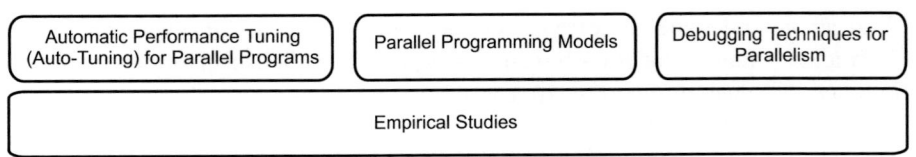

Fig. 2. Key areas of my multicore software engineering research.

3.1 Auto-Tuning

Performance is the main reason why we parallelize software. A complex parallel program can have many parameters influencing performance. Figure 3 (a) shows a biological data analysis application employing nested parallelism with tunable parameters on several layers [9]; for example, tunable parameters include the number of threads in different parts of the program, the size of various data structures that influences cache misses, but also the number of pipeline stages, the choice of algorithms and load-balancing techniques, or the number and size of data partitions that are processed in parallel.

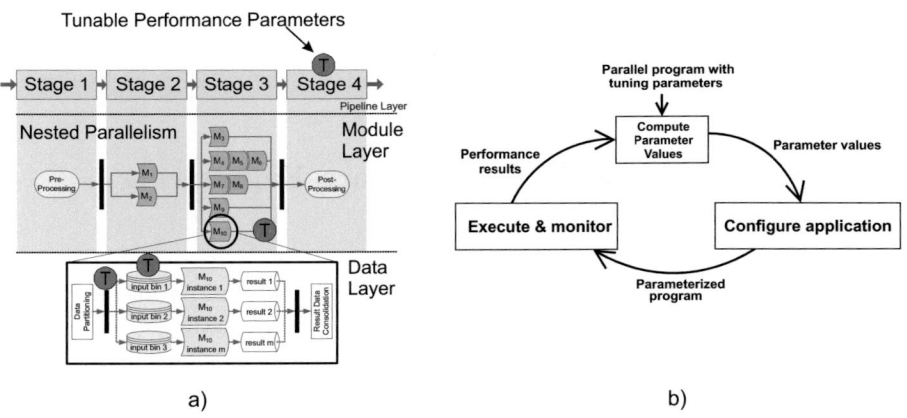

a)   b)

Fig. 3. (a) An example application with tunable performance parameters [9]; (b) Working principle of an auto-tuner based on [4].

Such parameters typically need to be adapted to the target hardware executing the program, because the characteristics of multicore platforms can vary, e.g., with respect to number of parallel hardware threads, cache architectures and sizes, memory bandwidth, or operating system. Adaptations are often done by hand and machine-dependent aspects are hard-coded to achieve best performance. This harms the portability of everyday software – imagine a user's disappointment of an application running fast on a laptop, but slow on a desktop PC. We cannot sacrifice portability in favor of performance.

This problem can be tackled using an auto-tuner, which is an external, dynamic optimizer working iteratively as shown in Figure 3 (b). In an offline tuning approach, a parallel application exposes tunable parameters, parameters ranges, as well as probes for feedback measurements to an auto-tuner. In one iteration, the auto-tuner calculates new parameter values, executes the application, and gathers feedback data. This cycle is repeated until some convergence criteria is satisfied (e.g., minimizing a given target function such as application run-time). The auto-tuning algorithms are a sub-area of my research.

We developed Atune-IL [11] as an instrumentation language to connect an auto-tuner to general-purpose multicore applications. A particular improvement are language features that exploit software architecture knowledge to avoid trying out unnecessary parameters combinations, thus significantly reducing the search space. Earlier experiments have also shown that fine-granular parallelism does not always provide enough leverage for good performance [9, 8]. As an improvement, we developed an approach to describe software architecture variants using parallel patterns; an auto-tuner finds the best parallel software architecture for a particular hardware platform [12].

My vision is that in the long-run, every application will be auto-tuned; every operating system will provide appropriate services and interfaces to make parallel application portability easy [4]. We successfully integrated an auto-tuner into the Linux operating system, which is capable of tuning several applications online while they are executing. In contrast to offline tuning, this approach can find the global, system-wide performance optimum. Important application scenarios include server applications, multimedia, games, and databases.

Why is auto-tuning important for software engineering? Because it separates performance tuning concerns from code development concerns. It can also find non-intuitive parameters values for the best performance. The tedious optimization is left to an auto-tuner, and programmers can write parallel code in a more generic way. Auto-Tuning will belong to the standard set of multicore software engineering tools, because it saves development time and improves portability. Parallel code becomes less complex, easier to read, understand, and maintain.

3.2 Parallel Programming Models

Programming models are a key area to improve developer's productivity and making parallelism easier to handle. Many industrial multicore applications have a complex structure and require the exploitation of several types of parallelism at the same time, such as task, data, or pipeline parallelism – very often in a nested fashion. In addition, current programming models have many pitfalls even for experts, leading to race conditions or deadlocks that go unnoticed for a long time.

One of my goals is to reduce the cognitive distance between the programmer's intentions and the actual implementation. I see a great potential in multi-paradigm languages; for example, declarative and imperative aspects can be combined in the same language to better handle parallelism and easily express programmer's thoughts. Declarative parts offer more potential for automatic performance tuning, while imperative parts offer more precise control. The ideologic disputes of the past – whether a functional, logic, or imperative approach is better for parallel programming – asked the wrong question; the real question is how to combine the best of all worlds in a meaningful way.

A particular direction I initiated and contributed to was the combination of stream-orientation with object-orientation in the XJava language [6, 5], which allows writing a Java program partly expressed in a stream-oriented way. Among others, introducing an operator similar to Unix pipes in Java makes the exploitation of pipeline parallelism easier and introduces new opportunities for automatic thread handling and tuning. Data parallelism can be automatically exploited through replication of stateless filters, and task parallelism can be deduced based on program structure. The new language constructs added to Java make parallel programming easier, because the potential to introduce parallel programming errors is reduced. For example, programmers don't have to care explicitly about buffers between pipeline stages, synchronization, or signalling; instead, they just use one operator.

3.3 Debugging Techniques for Parallelism

Debugging multicore programs is difficult because of nondeterministic executions; compared to sequential programs, developers also have to deal with race conditions and deadlocks.

The exact solution to finding all races in an arbitrary parallel program is equivalent to the halting problem. However, this is such an important field that we cannot afford to give up, so we need to work with heuristics. Of course, the accuracy of race detectors used at development time can be improved [3]. As all heuristics have trade-offs, I also approach this problem from additional angles: (1) already in the programming model, e.g., by introducing parallel constructs that don't allow too many wrong usages; (2) race detectors that work at run-time [13], after the application has been deployed in a productive environment. To be usable at run-time, our prototype online detector only selectively captures some of the most common race patters, but on the other hand it can automatically repair actually occurring races by delaying accesses of conflicting threads. (3) by employing data mining techniques on call graphs to detect, among others, wrong parallel program behavior that is caused by the wrong usage of non-parallel constructs [2]. This is a promising approach not only to automatically identify what causes incorrect results, but also what causes excessive resource usage (e.g., memory leaks) and performance degradation.

3.4 Empirical Studies

We are closely collaborating with industry partners to study novel applications areas for parallelism in realistic contexts with real data. The results show that multicore performance can indeed be successfully exploited in many scenarios.

For example, a parallelization of the route planner in one of SAP's business modules could reduce for real customer data (with hundreds of trucks and thousands of constraints) the computation time from hours to minutes. Other successes were achieved parallelizing a biological data analysis application, or extending Sun Microsystem's Electric Java application with parallel algorithms that speed up the placement optimization of cells on microchips. In other case studies, we parallelized a project management application, BZip compression, encryption (GnuPG), virus scanning (ClamAV), desktop search engines, and database query processing (PostgreSQL).

We also analyzed the potential and programmability of graphics cards for signal processing algorithms in an industrial context at Agilent, concluding that data parallelism can lead to significant speedups if the problems are suitable and have the right size, but that programmability and performance optimization are still a big obstacle. Other case studies used several teams working on the same programming problem, but with different programming approaches, e.g., Transactional Memory vs. Pthreads, or OpenMP vs. Pthreads; the results are summarized in [7, 8].

All studies show that despite the existing body of knowledge in parallel scientific computing, we need to extend our repertoire of tools for general-purpose parallel applications. Better software engineering support will benefit both scientific computing as well as everyday parallel programming.

4 Conclusion

Parallel computing has arrived on every desktop – it is not an exotic niche any more. These are exciting times for software engineering researchers, but also for practitioners to improve applications to scale their problem size and make innovative use of parallelism. The multicore approach has far-reaching implications for everyday applications that will go far beyond performance improvement. I envision that multiple cores will not be used to improve performance, but also to make everyday applications fault-tolerant and crash-proof, more secure, and to improve human-computer interaction in unprecedented ways.

Acknowledgments. Many thanks to the Excellence Initiative, the DFG, and the Landesstiftung Baden-Wuerttemberg for their support.

References

1. K. Asanovic et al. A view of the parallel computing landscape. *Commun. ACM*, 52(10):56–67, 2009.
2. F. Eichinger, V. Pankratius, P. W. L. Große, and K. Böhm. Localizing defects in multithreaded programs by mining dynamic call graphs. In *to appear in Proc. Testing: Academic & Industrial Conference Practice and Research Techniques*. Springer LNCS, 2010.
3. A. Jannesari, K. Bao, V. Pankratius, and W. Tichy. Helgrind+: An efficient dynamic race detector. In *IEEE International Symposium on Parallel Distributed Processing (IPDPS)*, pages 1 –13, 2009.

4. T. Karcher, C. Schaefer, and V. Pankratius. Auto-tuning support for manycore applications: perspectives for operating systems and compilers. *ACM SIGOPS Oper. Syst. Rev.*, 43(2):96–97, 2009.

5. F. Otto, V. Pankratius, and W. Tichy. High-level multicore programming with xjava. In *31st ACM/IEEE International Conference on Software Engineering*, pages 319 –322, 2009.

6. F. Otto, V. Pankratius, and W. Tichy. Xjava: Exploiting parallelism with object-oriented stream programming. In *Euro-Par 2009*, volume 5704 of *LNCS*, pages 875–886. Springer, 2009.

7. V. Pankratius, A.-R. Adl-Tabatabai, and F. Otto. Does transactional memory keep its promises? Results from an empirical study. Technical report, Technical Report 2009-12, IPD, University of Karlsruhe, Germany, September 2009.

8. V. Pankratius, A. Jannesari, and W. Tichy. Parallelizing bzip2: A case study in multicore software engineering. *Software, IEEE*, 26(6):70 –77, Nov.-Dec. 2009.

9. V. Pankratius, C. Schaefer, A. Jannesari, and W. F. Tichy. Software engineering for multicore systems: an experience report. In *Proc. ACM IWMSE '08*, pages 53–60, New York, NY, USA, 2008.

10. V. Pankratius and W. F. Tichy. Die Multicore-Revolution und ihre Bedeutung für die Softwareentwicklung. *Objektspektrum*, 4:30, 2008.

11. C. Schaefer, V. Pankratius, and W. Tichy. Atune-IL: An instrumentation language for auto-tuning parallel applications. In *Euro-Par 2009*, volume 5704 of *LNCS*, pages 9–20. Springer, 2009.

12. C. Schaefer, V. Pankratius, and W. F. Tichy. Engineering parallel applications with tunable architectures. In *Proc. of the 32nd ACM/IEEE International Conference on Software Engineering (ICSE 2010)*, Cape Town, South Africa, 2010.

13. J. Schimmel and V. Pankratius. Tachorace: Exploiting performance counters for run-time race detection. Technical report, Karlsruhe Institute of Technology, Technical Report 2010-01, 2010.

14. H. Sutter. The free lunch is over: A fundamental turn toward concurrency in software. *Dr. Dobb's Journal*, 30(3), 2005.

Biography. Dr. Pankratius heads since 2007 the Multicore Software Engineering young investigator group at KIT. He serves as the elected chairman of the "Software Engineering for Parallel Systems (SEPARS)" international working group that has more than 100 members. His current research concentrates on how to make parallel programming easier for the average programmer and covers a range of research topics including auto-tuning, language design, debugging, and empirical studies. Dr. Pankratius received for his work the Intel Leadership Award, the Sun Microsystems Concurrent Computing Community Award, and the Microsoft Research Faculty Fellowship Finalist Award. He received in 2007 a Ph.D. with distinction from the University of Karlsruhe, Germany, a Diplom degree (M.S.) in Business Computer Science best of class 2003 from the University of Münster, Germany, and a Bachelor of Science in Information Systems from the same university. He initiated and co-organized the series of Multicore Software Engineering workshops co-located with ICSE, the ACM/IEEE flagship conference on software engineering. He is a member of the ACM, IEEE, GI, and the elite program for postdocs of the Landesstiftung Baden-Wuerttemberg. Contact him at http://www.victorpankratius.com.

Engineering of Next Generation Self-Aware Software Systems: A Research Roadmap

Samuel Kounev

Institute for Program Structures and Data Organization (IPD)
Karlsruhe Institute of Technology (KIT)
76131 Karlsruhe, Germany
kounev@kit.edu

Abstract With the increasing adoption of virtualization and the transition towards cloud computing platforms, modern enterprise software systems are becoming increasingly complex and dynamic. The lack of direct control over the underlying physical hardware and the resulting gap between logical and physical resource allocations pose some major challenges in providing quality-of-service (QoS) guarantees. Due to the inability to automatically keep track of the complex interactions between the applications and workloads sharing the physical infrastructure, modern enterprise systems often exhibit poor QoS and resource efficiency, and have high operating costs. In this paper, we present a research roadmap and a long-term vision aiming to address these challenges. The presented research agenda is pursued by the Descartes Research Group at KIT which is funded by the German Research Foundation within the Emmy Noether Programme. Our long-term goal is to develop a novel methodology for engineering of next generation *self-aware* software systems. The latter will have built-in QoS models enhanced to capture dynamic aspects of the system environment and maintained automatically during operation. The models will be exploited at run-time to adapt the system to changes in the environment ensuring that resources are utilized efficiently and that QoS requirements are continuously satisfied.

1 Introduction

Modern enterprise systems based on the Service-Oriented Architecture (SOA) paradigm have highly distributed and dynamic architectures composed of loosely-coupled services that operate and evolve independently. Managing system resources in such environments to ensure acceptable end-to-end application quality-of-service (e.g., availability, performance and reliability) and efficient resource utilization is a challenge. The adoption of virtualization and cloud computing technologies, such as Software-as-a-Service (SaaS), Platform-as-a-Service (PaaS) and Infrastructure-as-a-Service (IaaS), comes at the cost of increased system complexity and dynamicity. The increased complexity is caused by the introduction of virtual resources and the resulting gap between logical and physical resource allocations. The increased dynamicity is caused by the complex interactions between the applications and workloads sharing the physical infrastructure. The inability to predict such interactions and adapt the system accordingly makes it hard to provide quality-of-service (QoS) guarantees in terms of availability and responsiveness, as well as resilience to attacks and operational failures. Moreover, the consolidation of workloads translates into higher utilization of physical resources which makes the system much more vulnerable to threats resulting from unforeseen load fluctuations, hardware failures and network attacks.

Service providers are often faced with questions such as: What QoS would a new service deployed on the virtualized infrastructure exhibit and how much resources should be allocated to it? What would be the effect of migrating a service from one virtual machine (VM) to another? How should the system configuration be adapted to avoid QoS issues or inefficient resource usage arising from changing customer workloads? Answering such questions requires the ability to predict at *run-time* how the QoS of running services and applications would be affected if the system configuration or the workload changes. We refer to this as *online QoS prediction*. Due to the inability to automatically keep track of dynamic changes in the system environment and predict their effect, SOA systems in use nowadays often exhibit poor QoS and resource efficiency, and have high operating costs. To accommodate load fluctuations, services are typically hosted on dedicated servers with over-provisioned capacity. Servers in data centers nowadays typically run at around 20% utilization [11] which corresponds to their lowest energy-efficiency region [2]. The growing number of under-utilized servers, often referred to as "server sprawl", translates into increasing data center operating costs including power consumption costs, cooling infrastructure costs and system management costs. To counter this development, novel methods for online QoS prediction and autonomic resource management are needed.

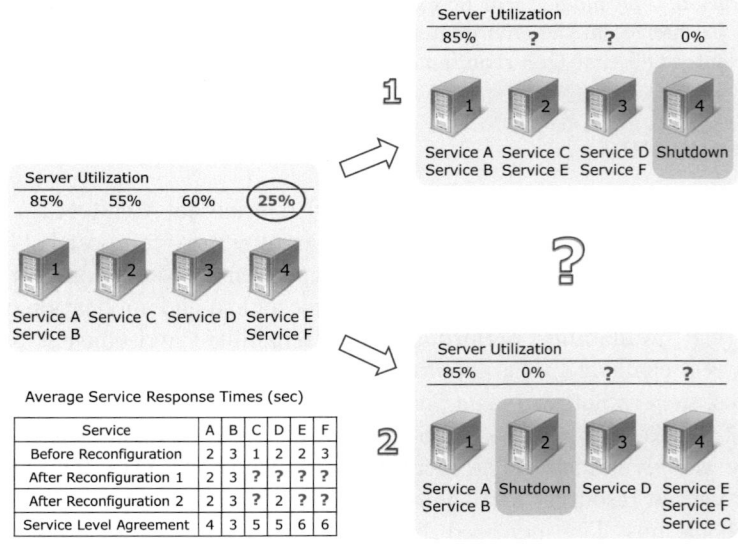

Figure 1. Online QoS Prediction Scenario

To illustrate how online QoS prediction can help to improve the system resource efficiency, we consider a simple example depicted in Figure 1. A SOA system made of four servers hosting six different services is shown including information on the average service response times, the response time service level agreements (SLAs) and the server utilization. Now assume that due to a change in the demand for services E and F, the average utilization of the fourth server has dropped down to 25% over an extended period of time. To improve the resource efficiency, it is considered to shut down one of the servers migrating its services to other servers. Two possible ways to reconfigure the system (shutting down the second and the fourth server respectively) are shown. To ensure that reconfiguring the system would not break the SLAs, the system needs a mechanism to predict the effect of the reconfiguration on the service response times. Given that this must be done at run-time, online QoS prediction capabilities are required.

In the rest of this paper, we present the research agenda and long-term vision of a research project carried out by the Descartes Research Group at KIT aiming to address the challenges described above.

2   Research Agenda and Long-Term Vision

The Descartes Research Group [1] at KIT was started in July 2009 and is funded by the German Research Foundation (DFG) within the Emmy Noether Programme. The group is working on novel approaches to software and systems engineering that ensure that non-functional QoS requirements are continuously satisfied during operation while at the same time infrastructure resources are utilized efficiently lowering the system TCO (Total-Cost-of-Ownership). The research areas and technology domains we are focusing on are depicted in Figure 2.

Our research is divided into three main areas: i) system design, measurement and analysis targeted at understanding the system behavior and the way it is influenced by the environment it is running in, ii) system modeling for QoS prediction both at system design-time and during operation, and iii) autonomic and self-adaptive system QoS management. The three areas are closely interrelated. On the one hand, building representative models requires deep understanding of the system behavior as well as measurement data to calibrate the models. On the other hand, methods for self-adaptive QoS management rely on predictive models that help to predict the effect of adaptation decisions at run-time.

Our long-term research agenda aims at developing a novel methodology for engineering of so-called *self-aware* software systems [7]. The latter will have built-in online QoS prediction and self-adaptation capabilities addressing the challenges described in Section 1. This vision is the major topic of our research group which is named after the French philosopher and mathematician René Descartes. Self-awareness in this context is meant in the sense that systems should be aware of changes that occur in their environment and should be able to predict the effect of such changes on their QoS (*"thought is what happens in me such that I am immediately conscious of it"* – René Descartes). Furthermore,

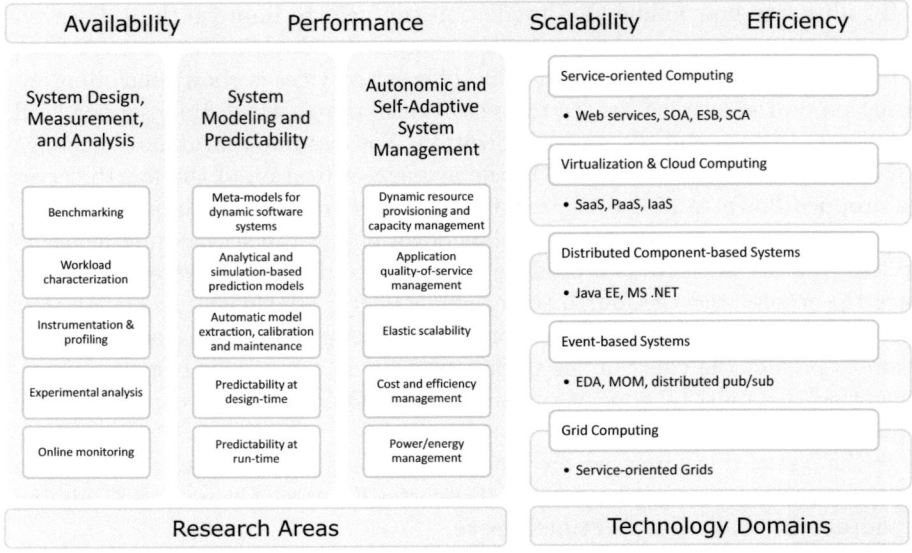

Figure 2. Research Areas and Technology Domains

systems should automatically adapt as the environment evolves in order to ensure that infrastructure resources are utilized efficiently and QoS requirements are continuously satisfied (*"for it is not enough to have a good mind: one must use it well" – René Descartes*). To realize this vision, we advocate the use of *dynamic QoS models* integrated into the system components and used at runtime for online QoS prediction. The models will serve as a "mind" to the system controlling its behavior, i.e., resource allocations and scheduling decisions. In analogy to Descartes' *dualism principle* (*"the mind controls the body, but the body can also influence the mind"*), the link between the QoS models and the system components they represent will be bidirectional.

The new dynamic QoS models will be designed to encapsulate all information, both static and dynamic, relevant to predicting a service's QoS on-the-fly. This includes information about the service's software architecture, its workload and its execution environment. Current architecture-level[1] performance models for component-based architectures, surveyed in [8], (e.g., PCM [3], CBML [12], CB-SPE [4]) will be used as a basis. The latter will be extended to capture the performance influences of the platforms used at each layer of the service execution environment focusing on the virtualization and middleware layers. Resource

---

[1] We distinguish between *descriptive* architecture-level QoS models and *predictive* QoS models. The former describe QoS-relevant aspects of software architectures and execution environments (e.g., UML models augmented with QoS-related annotations). The latter capture the temporal system behavior and can be used for QoS prediction by means of analytical or simulation techniques (e.g., Markov chains, layered queueing networks or stochastic Petri nets).

allocations at the different layers will be modeled explicitly and benchmark results will be exploited to quantify the relative performance of different execution platforms. This will make it possible to predict how the QoS of a running service will be affected if resource allocations are modified or if the service is migrated from one VM to another possibly running on a different platform.

Unlike conventional architecture-level QoS models, the developed models will be *dynamic* in the sense that they will be maintained and updated automatically to reflect the evolving system environment. To realize this, execution platforms should be enhanced with functionality to automatically extract and maintain the models during operation. Depending on the type of system considered and the availability of monitoring and instrumentation frameworks, the degree of automation of the initial model extraction will be different. For example, for a newly developed system, the model extraction could potentially be completely automated, whereas for legacy systems some manual steps might be required.

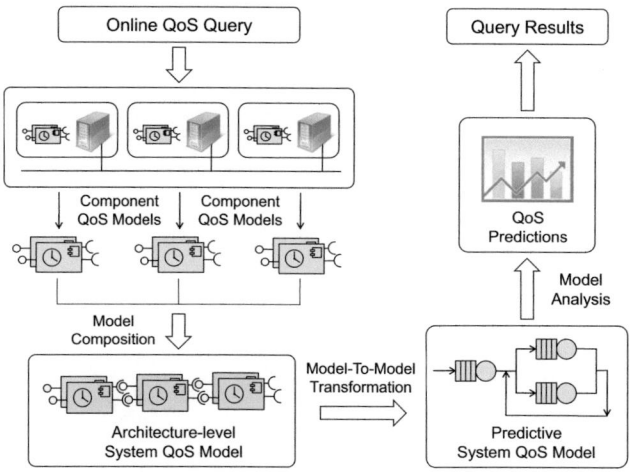

Figure 3. Online QoS Prediction Process

The dynamic QoS models will be used during operation to answer QoS-related queries such as: What would be the effect on the QoS of running applications if a new application is deployed in the virtualized environment or an existing application is migrated from one server to another? How much resources need to be allocated to a newly deployed application to ensure that service-level agreements (SLAs) are satisfied? What QoS would the system exhibit after a period of time if the workload continues to develop according to the current trends? How should the system configuration be adapted to avoid QoS problems or inefficient resource usage arising from changing customer workloads? We refer to such queries as *online QoS queries*.

Figure 3 illustrates the process that will be followed in order to provide an answer to a query. First, the QoS models of all involved system components will be retrieved and combined by means of model composition techniques into a single architecture-level QoS model encapsulating all information relevant to answering the QoS query. This model will then be transformed into a predictive QoS model by means of an automatic *model-to-model transformation*. Existing model-to-model transformations for static architecture-level performance models will be used as a basis, e.g., [3, 9]. The target predictive model type and level of abstraction as well as the solution technique will be determined on-the-fly based on the required accuracy and the time available for the analysis. Multiple model types (e.g., layered queueing networks, stochastic process algebras, queueing Petri nets and general-purpose simulation models) and model solution techniques (e.g., exact analytical techniques, numerical approximation techniques, simulation and bounding techniques) will be used in order to provide flexibility in trading-off between prediction accuracy and analysis overhead.

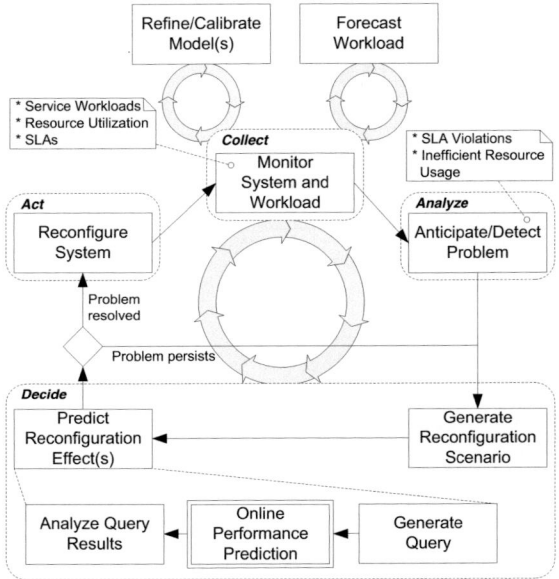

Figure 4. Online Reconfiguration Process

The ability to answer online QoS queries during operation will provide the basis for implementing techniques for self-aware QoS management. Such techniques will be triggered automatically during operation in response to observed or forecast changes in application workloads. The goal will be to proactively adapt the system to such changes in order to avoid anticipated QoS problems or inefficient resource usage. The adaptation will be performed in an autonomic fashion by considering a set of possible system reconfiguration scenarios (e.g, changing VM placement and/or resource allocations) and exploiting the online QoS query mechanism to predict the effect of such reconfigurations before making a decision. Figure 4 depicts the online reconfiguration process and the self-adaptation control loop. The latter is based on the generic model of a control loop from [6] which we have extended to integrate the use of the online QoS query mechanism. In addition to the main control loop, two additional loops are running in the background, one for continuously refining and calibrating online models and one for forecasting the workload evolution.

As an initial step towards the described vision, we conducted two preliminary case studies. In the first case study, we studied a complex Java EE application showing how detailed architecture-level performance models can be extracted and maintained automatically at run-time based on online monitoring data [5]. As a performance model we used the Palladio Component Model [3]. The extracted performance models provided performance predictions with less than 30% deviation from measurements on the real system. In the second case study, we studied a SOA application running in a service-oriented Grid computing environment [10] and showed how online performance models (based on hierarchical queueing Petri nets) can be used at run-time for autonomic QoS-aware resource allocation. The case studies demonstrate that the existing gap between architecture-level QoS models and run-time QoS management can be closed.

3   Concluding Remarks

Modern enterprise systems based on the SOA paradigm have highly distributed and dynamic architectures composed of loosely-coupled services often deployed in virtualized computing infrastructures. Managing system resources in such environments to ensure acceptable end-to-end application quality-of-service and efficient resource utilization is a challenge. In this paper, we presented a research roadmap and a long-term vision aiming to address this challenge. The presented research agenda is pursued by the Descartes Research Group at KIT which is working towards the development of a novel methodology for engineering of next generation *self-aware* software systems. Such systems will be aware of their QoS and the way it is affected by the environment they are running in. Moreover, they will automatically adapt as the environment evolves ensuring that system resources are utilized efficiently and QoS requirements are continuously satisfied. The described approach raises several big challenges that represent emerging hot topics in the software engineering community and will be subject of long-term fundamental research in the years to come. The resolution of these challenges promises to revolutionize the field of systems engineering and radically transform the way enterprise systems are built and managed. The introduced self-awareness and autonomous management will provide a number of benefits such as better quality-of-service, lower operating costs and improved energy efficiency.

4   Short Biographical Sketch

Dr.-Ing. Samuel Kounev is head of the Descartes Research Group at Karlsruhe Institute of Technology (KIT). He received a MSc degree in mathematics and computer science from the University of Sofia (1999) and a PhD degree in computer science from Technische Universität Darmstadt (2005). From February 2006 to May 2008, he was a research fellow at Cambridge University working in the systems research group of Prof. Jean Bacon at the Computer Laboratory. In April 2009, he received the Emmy-Noether Career award from the German Research Foundation (DFG) and started the Descartes Research Group at KIT. Dr. Kounev's research is focused on methods for autonomic management of system quality-of-service (e.g., availability, performance and reliability) and resource efficiency (e.g., energy consumption) throughout the system life-cycle. Dr. Kounev is founder of the SPEC International Performance Evaluation Workshop (SIPEW) and co-founder of the ACM/SPEC International Conference on Performance Engineering (ICPE). He served as a BEA Technical Director from 2004 to 2008 and as a release manager of SPEC's Java Subcommittee from 2003 to 2009. During this time he led the development and standardization of several widely adopted industry-standard benchmarks including SPECjAppServer2004, SPECjms2007 and SPECjbb2005. He is a member of the ACM, IEEE, and the GI e.V.

References

1. Descartes Project Website. http://www.descartes-research.net, 2010.
2. L. A. Barroso and U. Hölzle. The Case for Energy-Proportional Computing. *IEEE Computer*, 40(12):33–37, 2007.
3. S. Becker, H. Koziolek, and R. Reussner. The Palladio component model for model-driven performance prediction. *Journal of Syst. and Softw.*, 82:3–22, 2009.
4. A. Bertolino and R. Mirandola. Software Performance Engineering of Component-based Systems. In *Proc. of WOSP-2004*. ACM Press, 2004.
5. F. Brosig, S. Kounev, and K. Krogmann. Automated Extraction of Palladio Component Models from Running Enterprise Java Applications. In *Proc. of ROSSA-2009*. ACM, 2009.
6. B. H. C. Cheng, R. de Lemos, H. Giese, P. Inverardi, and J. Magee. Software Engineering for Self-Adaptive Systems: A Research Roadmap. In *Software Engineering for Self-Adaptive Systems, LNCS 5525*, pages 1–26, 2009.
7. S. Kounev, F. Brosig, N. Huber, and R. Reussner. Towards self-aware performance and resource management in modern service-oriented systems. In *Proceedings of the 7th IEEE International Conference on Services Computing (SCC 2010), July 5-10, Miami, Florida, USA*. IEEE Computer Society, 2010.
8. H. Koziolek. Performance evaluation of component-based software systems: A survey. *Perform. Eval.*, In Press, 2009.
9. H. Koziolek and R. Reussner. A Model Transformation from the Palladio Component Model to Layered Queueing Networks. In *Proc. of SIPEW-2008*. Springer LNCS 5119, 2008.
10. R. Nou, S. Kounev, F. Julia, and J. Torres. Autonomic QoS control in enterprise Grid environments using online simulation. *Journal of Systems and Software*, 82:486–502, 2009.
11. K. Parent. Server Consolidation Improves IT's Capacity Utilization. Vol. 2006: Court Square Data Group, 2005.
12. X. Wu and M. Woodside. Performance Modeling from Software Components. In *Proc. of WOSP-2004*, pages 290–301. ACM Press, January 2004.

Checking Software Reliability

Mana Taghdiri

Institute of Theoretical Informatics
mana.taghdiri@kit.edu

Abstract. The research group "Automated Software Analysis" at the institute for Theoretical Informatics at KIT aims at developing techniques for checking software reliability automatically. The goal is to develop techniques that are scalable, easy to use, and therefore, can be applied to real-world software systems.

1 Problem Statement

As software systems grow in size and complexity, it becomes increasingly difficult to develop and maintain reliable software. Reports suggest that software failures have caused aerospace, medical, and banking industries to lose billions of dollars, and hundreds of lives [13]. Employing automatic techniques to improve software reliability reduces not only the cost of development, but also the risk of catastrophic failures.

The goal of our research group – Automated Software Analysis – is to improve software reliability by developing automatic techniques that increase programmers' confidence in their developed systems. In recent years, a lot of progress has been made in this direction. Techniques such as software model checking, automatic test case generation, and automatic invariant extraction have been successfully used as means of detecting errors in programs. However, despite all advances, automatically checking deep semantic properties of software systems remains a challenging problem. Existing techniques (e.g. theorem proving) that can handle rich properties often require extensive user assistance, and thus, are costly to apply to large programs. On the other hand, fully automatic techniques (e.g. shallow static analyses) that are scalable cannot handle rich properties.

Our research attempts to bridge this gap. It provides a suite of fully automatic analysis techniques that can handle deep behavioral properties of *structure-rich* software. Examples of such software include programs with object-oriented design, where the program behavior depends on the configuration of the objects stored in the heap. *Deep* properties are not necessarily complex properties; they are the ones that involve linked data structures and thus can be specified only using the full power of an expressive logic. For example, in order to specify that the elements stored in the key column of a database are unique, a notion of reachability as well as nested quantiers are required.

Checking structure-rich programs is particularly important because erroneous manipulations of data structures may cause loss and/or unauthorized access of data, and may eventually cause a system to crash. On the other hand, since linked data structures can get arbitrarily complex, it is often too hard to check their validity by traditional testing techniques. Thus, our main focus is to develop automatic techniques to help users check and understand how a program manipulates complex data structures.

We target two of the main challenges in checking structure-rich software: scalability and full automation. In order to make a software analysis technique applicable to real-life software systems, it is important for the technique to scale to large pieces of software, and to require little effort from the user. That is, an ideal technique will run at a *push of a button*. To achieve this goal, we have sacrificed completeness: the techniques that we develop aim at *finding bugs* in software systems, rather than proving them correct. However, although they don't guarantee software correctness in general, they provide an arguably better alternative to traditional testing practices.

The rest of this paper gives a brief description of our recent projects and future directions.

2   Checking Design-level Requirements

An active project in our group is to develop frameworks for checking software properties at the design level, and thus, to find semantic bugs before the system is actually implemented. Our design-level analysis is based on constraint solving: characteristics of the analyzed system are specified as logical constraints and checked against the requirements using a constraint solver. The level of abstraction is chosen by the user and affects the scalability of the approach.

2.1   Formal Analysis of a Network Protocol

We have developed a framework [15] for modeling and checking the design of a class of key management schemes used in secure multicast protocols. The framework is constructed in Alloy [8], a lightweight relational modeling language, and aims at checking key management schemes against some critical correctness properties that should be satisfied by all secure multicast protocols. The proposed framework introduces a novel idiom for modeling distributed systems. Compared to the conventional way of modeling these systems, this idiom is simpler and more intuitive, while supporting better modularity.

We used the developed framework to model pull-based ARF and Iolus, two very different schemes addressing the scalability issue involved in the group key management problem. The models were then analyzed using the Alloy Analyzer, a fully automatic simulation and checking tool for Alloy models. The analyses exposed some flaws, including one security breach in ARF, previously unknown to its designers. Although the models of these protocols are abstract, we have been careful to remain faithful enough to ensure that all the scenarios made by the Alloy Analyzer are in fact real, so that flaws detected actually exist in the protocol.

Our experience supports the contention that lightweight formal methods are feasible and economical. Our model of ARF, for example, is less than 100 lines of code in its entirety, and yet it exposed significant flaws previously unknown to its designers.

2.2 Developing a Constraint Solver

Based on our experience with the Alloy analyzer, we are currently developing a new constraint solver that is capable of analyzing the logical formulas that arise when describing structure-rich systems. The constraint solver will be suitable for checking both data structure specifications and numerical properties. It will be a fully-automatic, stand-alone tool that can be employed as the analysis engine in a variety of settings.

Alloy [8] is a first order, declarative language that is widely used for specifying safety properties of structure-rich systems. It is based on relational logic and supports transitive closure as a built-in language construct. Due to its expressiveness and yet simplicity, Alloy has been used in a wide range of applications, both as a stand-alone constraint solver (e.g [1, 9, 12]), and as a backend engine in various program analysis tools (e.g [4, 10, 16]).

Capabilities such as nested quantification, set comprehension, typed expressions, and a transitive closure operator make Alloy an expressive language, and particularly well-suited for expressing rich properties. However, since Alloy formulas are translated to propositional logic and solved by a SAT solver, Alloy provides limited support for integers, arithmetic expressions, and arrays, restricting analysis of systems with numerical computations.

Several constraint solvers have been developed that can check arithmetic constraints. SAT modulo theory (SMT) solvers (e.g. [5, 11]) are particularly attractive because they efficiently support a rich combination of background theories such as integer arithmetic, uninterpreted functions, theories of arrays and list structures, and the theory of bit vectors.

In this project, we will develop a new constraint solver that preserves the advantages of the two approaches: it supports a first order relational logic with transitive closure (similar to Alloy), but uses an SMT solver to check its satisfiability. Consequently, the solver will be capable of handling both structural and numerical constraints and thus, will potentially support a wide range of applications.

In order to evaluate the feasibility of this approach, we have performed a case study [7] in which an SMT solver, namely Yices [5], is used to analyze different variations of an Alloy problem. Our analysis generalizes the Alloy analysis by taking advantage of the background theories available in Yices, and avoiding type finitization when possible. Our experimental results are very encouraging. Out of a total of 9 properties checked, 5 could be verified by Yices without having to finitize any of the types, meaning that we could soundly prove them correct – a capability completely missing from the Alloy Analyzer. Furthermore, in most cases, our analysis out-performed Alloy in terms of runtime.

3 Checking Code-level Properties

In addition to our work on design-level software checking, we develop techniques for checking safety properties of software systems at the implementation level. The techniques are static, fully automatic, and require very little input from the user. Similar to our design-level work, these techniques are also based on constraint solving, and mainly use the Alloy language to express the intermediate logical constraints.

3.1 Specification Extraction

Modular program analysis techniques work by decomposing a large program into smaller parts whose behaviors can be expressed succinctly using specifications, and combining those specifications to determine the behavior of the program as a whole. Traditional modular techniques require users to provide such specifications. However, this requirement puts too much burden on users and often limits the applicability of those techniques. Thus, the focus is shifting to generating modules specifications automatically (see e.g. [6, 17, 19]).

Since automatically extracting the full specification of an arbitrary piece of code is infeasible, generated specifications usually *approximate* the behavior of their corresponding modules. While some techniques have been developed to generate specifications in the context of temporal safety properties, generating specifications suitable for checking data structure properties in a large program still remains a challenge.

We have developed a lightweight, flow-sensitive, context-sensitive technique [17] for extracting syntactic specifications from an object-oriented program. The goal is to generate specifications that (1) safely abstract the behavior of procedures, (2) are suitable for checking data structure properties in large programs, and (3) are readable by both tools and users. Our technique is sound, static, fully-automatic, and produces specifications in the Alloy logic.

The key idea is an abstract interpretation [3] in which a procedure is evaluated symbolically, where each statement updates the set of possible values for each field and variable. The values are approximated using Alloy expressions. When the analysis terminates, the extracted specification abstracts the behavior of the procedure by specifying both an upper and a lower bound on the final value of each field and variable mutated by that procedure. Our experiments show that this technique is quick and scalable, and in many cases, results in specifications that are accurate enough to prove detailed data structure properties about complex heap-manipulating programs; only in a few cases was there a significant loss of information. These results suggest that this analysis represents a useful balance between tractability and accuracy.

3.2 Checking Code without Specifications

We have introduces a novel approach to checking data structure properties in object-oriented programs [16]. Unlike previous attempts for checking this class of properties, our technique mainly aims at scalability and full automation. To that end, we have developed a modular technique that does not require any user interaction or user-provided annotations beyond provision of the property to check.

The key insight behind this approach is that in order to check a large program with respect to a property, it is often sufficient to consider only a small subset of the code; the rest can be abstracted away. Our technique computes such abstractions automatically. That is, it automatically infers some context-dependent specifications from the code that are sufficient to check the validity of a property. This eliminates the need for user-provided intermediate annotations, a major obstacle in applying existing techniques to large programs.

Building on the results from the previous project, this bug finding technique works by automatically inferring specifications for each procedure call. The inferred specifications are context-dependent: their precision depends on both the calling context in which they are being used and the property being checked. As a result, a very partial specification is sometimes sufficient, because even though it barely captures the behavior of the called procedure, it nevertheless captures enough to verify the caller.

The specifications are inferred iteratively as needed, following the counterexample guided abstraction refinement framework [2]. The analysis starts by substituting some rough initial specification for each called procedure (extracted by the technique of the previous project). These specifications are later refined in response to spurious counterexamples. Thus, only as much information about a procedure is analyzed as is needed to check the property.

Karun, the prototype tool that we have developed, uses Alloy as the specification language, and Kodkod [18], an Alloy model finder, as the constraint solver. It targets Java programs and performs the analysis with respect to a bounded heap. Karun uses an abstract interpretation technique [17] to produce initial summaries of procedure calls, which are then used to compute an Alloy formula that encodes the initial abstraction of the code. Kodkod checks the generated formula with respect to the property of interest by translating it to a propositional formula and using an off-the-shelf SAT solver to find a counterexample. Found counterexamples are then checked for validity, again using a SAT solver. If the counterexample is invalid, the solver will generate an unsatisfiable core [20] (a witness to unsatisfiability) which will then be converted to a refined specification. This process continues until either a valid counterexample is found, or the property is shown to be valid with respect to the analyzed domain. Since the analysis is performed with respect to a bounded domain, it cannot prove the correctness of the program. It is only suited for finding bugs. However, the analyzed domain is checked exhaustively. That is, if a counterexample exists within that domain, it is guaranteed to be found.

Karun handles only a basic subset of the Java language, and thus, we have performed our feasibility study only on small portions of some open source programs. The results, however, were very encouraging. We managed to find two previously unknown bugs – categorized as "major" – in Quartz – a widely used, open source job scheduling software. Furthermore, our technique could handle very complex data structure properties, and could check an order of magnitude larger programs than a technique that inlined called procedures – the only other approach possible in the absence of any user-provided annotations.

4 Future Directions

The main challenge of our work is to make our analysis techniques scale to larger pieces of software. With that goal in mind, we will continue working on both our design-level and our code-level projects, investigating various fundamental ideas, and evaluating their effects.

4.1 Constraint Solving

Our project on developing a constraint solver based on SMT solving is a long term project that involves efficient translation of the whole Alloy language to an SMT solver language. This is particularly challenging because Alloy includes several undecidable constructs whose translations require experiments with various equivalent formulas to find one that best suites all application contexts.

In order to improve the usability of our solver, we have to ensure that it provides useful feedback to users. When an SMT solver determines that a formula is satisfiable, it returns a satisfying instance of the formula. Similarly, if the formula is unsatisfiable, some SMT solvers (e.g. [5]) can produce an unsatisfiable core [20] – a generally small unsatisfiable subset of the input clauses that proves the unsatisfiability of the whole formula.

Such information vastly improve the usability of any constraint solver. A satisfying model helps the user detect under-specification whereas an unsat core helps him detect over-specification [14]. Our constraint solver will incorporate techniques for communicating models and cores back to the user. That is, satisfying models will be mapped back to symbolic values of the relations in the original formula, and clauses in an unsatisfiable core will be translated back to the subexpressions and subformulas that generated them in the first place.

4.2 Specification Languages

An important problem in applying static program checking techniques to real software is that their specification languages either do not have a well-defined semantics or are not intuitive enough for users. Karun – our current prototype tool for checking code conformance – for example, assumes that the property of interest is expressed in terms of the data structures used in the code under analysis. That is, analyzed properties are code-level specifications, not high level requirements.

Our experiments show that writing such low level properties, even for people familiar with the details of the code, is laborious and error-prone. Designing semantically-consistent specification patterns and abstract datatypes can substantially improve the usability of the analysis.

4.3 Checking Code Conformance

While our initial work on checking safety properties of structure-rich programs looks very promising, it provides insight into the problems that should be addressed in order to make the approach work on large software systems.

Our intermediate logic, Alloy, is uniquely suitable for expressing complex data structure properties. However, it offers a limited support for integer arithmetic, and thus, array access analysis. In fact, because numerical expressions in Karun are converted to a propositional logic by bit blasting, they can be analyzed with respect to only a small bitwidth (usually much smaller than the actual bitwidth used by the compilers). As a result, counterexamples that involve numerical expressions may be false alarms. This is currently the only source of false alarms in Karun, and can be eliminated by a better choice of the underlying constraint solver. We expect that compared to a SAT solver, a Sat Modulo Theory (SMT) solver be better suited for finding bugs in real programs that contain both linked data structures, and numerical expressions and arrays.

4.4 Domain-specific Analysis

While a general-purpose analysis can potentially be applied to software in various domains, it can always benefit from domain-specific knowledge. We are particularly interested to study how our counterexample-guided abstraction refinement (CEGAR) technique can be applied to the software security domain. More specifically, we are using a CEGAR-based approach to check whether a program contains an illegal flow of information or not. The initial examples, worked out manually, promise feasibility and effectiveness. Further experiments will be performed once the idea is implemented as an automatic tool.

References

1. Mondex case study. http://www.eleves.ens.fr/home/ramanana/work/mondex.
2. E. Clarke, O. Grumberg, S. Jha, Y. Lu, and H. Veith. Counterexample-guided abstraction refinement. In *International conference on computer-aided verification*, pages 154–169, 2000.
3. P. Cousot and R. Cousot. Abstract interpretation: a unified lattice model for static analysis of programs by construction or approximation of fixpoints. In *Symposium on Principles of Programming Languages*, pages 238–252, 1977.
4. G. Dennis, F. Chang, and D. Jackson. Modular verification of code with SAT. In *International Symposium on Software Testing and Analysis*, pages 109–120, 2006.
5. B. Dutertre and L. Moura. The yices smt solver. Technical report, SRI International, 2006.
6. C. Flanagan and K. Leino. Houdini, an annotation assistant for ESC/Java. In *International symposium of formal methods Europe*, pages 500–517, 2001.
7. A. El Ghazi and M. Taghdiri. Analyzing alloy formulas using an smt solver: A case study. In *Automated Formal Methods (AFM)*, 2010.
8. D. Jackson. *Software Abstractions: Logic, Language, and Analysis*. The MIT Press, 2006.

9. E. Kang and D. Jackson. Formal modeling and analysis of a flash filesystem in alloy. In *International Conference on Abstract State Machine, Alloy, B and Z*, 2008.

10. S. Khurshid. *Generating Structurally Complex Tests from Declarative Constraints.* PhD thesis, MIT, 2003.

11. L. De Moura and N. Bjorner. Z3: An efficient smt solver. In *Conference on Tools and Algorithms for the Construction and Analysis of Systems*, 2008.

12. S. Narain, G. Levin, V. Kaul, and S. Malik. Declarative infrastructure configuration synthesis and debugging. In *JNSM*, 2008.

13. Collection of Software Bugs. `http://www5.in.tum.de/~huckle/bugse.html`.

14. I. Shlyakhter, R. Seater, D. Jackson, M. Sridharan, and M. Taghdiri. Debugging declarative models using unsatisfiable core. In *International Conference on Automated Software Engineering*, pages 94–105, 2003.

15. M. Taghdiri and D. Jackson. A lightweight formal analysis of a multicast key management scheme. In *International Conference on Formal Techniques for Networked and Distributed Systems*, pages 240–256, 2003.

16. M. Taghdiri and D. Jackson. Inferring specifications to detect errors in code. *Journal of Automated Software Engineering*, 14(1):87–121, 2007.

17. M. Taghdiri, R. Seater, and D. Jackson. Lightweight extraction of syntactic specifications. In *International Symposium on Foundations of Software Engineering*, pages 276–286, 2006.

18. E. Torlak and D. Jackson. Kodkod: A relational model finder. In *International conference on tools and algorithms for construction and analysis of systems*, pages 632–647, 2007.

19. Y. Xie and A. Aiken. Scalable error detection using boolean satisfiability. In *Symposium on principles of programming languages*, pages 351–363, 2005.

20. L. Zhang and S. Malik. Validating SAT solvers using an independent resolution-based checker: practical implementations and other applications. In *Design, Automation and Test in Europe*, pages 10880–10886, 2003.

Author's biography

Mana Taghdiri is a junior professor of the Institute for Theoretical Informatics at the department of computer science, Karlsruhe Institute of Technology. She leads the Automated Software Analysis research group which focuses on developing lightweight techniques for checking software reliability. She has received two ACM/SIGSOFT distinguished paper awards for her work on reducing user's efforts in checking software safety characteristics. Dr. Taghdiri received her Ph.D. and Masters degrees in computer science from Massachusetts Institute of Technology in 2007 and 2002, respectively, and her Bachelors degree from Sharif University of Technology in 2001. Prior to joining KIT, she was a senior software engineer at The MathWorks, Inc, designing a just-in-time compiler for the MATLAB language. She can be reached via email at `mana.taghdiri@kit.edu` or telephone at +49 721 608-5893.

Software Verification:
State of the Art and Challenges
Illustrated on the Problem of Malware Protection

Carsten Sinz

Research Group "Verification Meets Algorithm Engineering"
Institute for Theoretical Computer Science
Karlsruhe Institut of Technology
carsten.sinz@kit.edu   http://verialg.iti.uka.de

Abstract. We give an overview on the state of the art in software verification, and illustrate it on an application of substantial importance: avoidance of security leaks in programs.

1 Introduction

Software verification, i.e. ascertening properties of software with the quality of a mathematical proof, is considered one of the great challenges in computer science. First ideas go back to Turing [9], or even to Leibniz, who proposed to use machines to resolve disputes by *computing* the right answer:

> The only way to rectify our reasonings is to make them as tangible as those of the Mathematicians, so that we can find our error at a glance, and when there are disputes among persons, we can simply say: Let us calculate (*calculemus*), without further ado, to see who is right.[1]

In the 60s of the 20th century the theoretical ground was laid for many of the theoretical foundations for verification of programs. However, it took until the beginning of this century to see these ideas become applicable in practice. In 2002, Bill Gates called software verification the *Holy Grail of Computer Science*, and saw first steps towards verifying real software being accomplished.

In this article we will give an overview on software verification methods and illustrate them on one particular application of substantial importance: avoidance of security leaks in programs.

2 How to Protect Computer Systems?

Todays computer systems are exposed to a multitude of threats from the Internet: data theft, malware intrusion, hacker attacks, or espionage are among the most common. The damage caused by these attacks is considerable: Technology research firm Computer Economics Inc. estimates the worldwide damage caused by malware (i.e. viruses, worms, Trojan horses) to 13.3 billion in 2006.[2] In a study conducted by *Pricewater-*

---

[1] G. W. Leibniz, The Art of Discovery; 1685.

[2] http://www.computereconomics.com/article.cfm?id=1225.

houseCoopers it is stated that hacker attacks cost the world economy a whopping 1.6 trillion in 2000. Most of these attacks are rendered possible by software errors, which permit intrusion of malicious software (malware) that is secretly installed on a computer. Malware can then take control over the computer system in many unwanted ways, e.g., to make the system participate in a Distributed Denial of Service attack (DDoS). This also happened during the cyber-attacks targeted against Estonia in the first two weeks of May 2007, where the government was affected as well as banking, media and police sites.[3]

Among the software errors exploited for such attacks, buffer overflow and integer overflow errors are the most common. The Vulnerability Trends 2006 report (published in May 2007 by CVE-MITRE) states:[4]

> Buffer overflows are still the number one issue as reported in operating system (OS) vendor advisories. (...) Integer overflows, barely in the top ten overall in the past few years, are number two for OS vendor advisories (in 2006), behind buffer overflows.

Many of the upcoming attacks against virtualized servers (hypervisor-malware) are also based on overflow errors. Security expert Rafal Mojtczuk mentioned, e.g., in his talk about the hypervisor Xen on the Blackhat Conference in August 2008 that "far-reaching attacks are possible due to multiple (...) integer overflow errors in Linux ext2 file system utilities."[5] It is thus of utmost importance to come to a higher level of software quality with fewer exploitable errors.

Over the last years, considerable progress has been made in detecting and avoiding software errors. Methods like static analysis or different techniques of software verification have been developed and are already adopted by companies developing security critical applications, e.g., in the automotive or avionics industry. However, the tools currently available still suffer from substantial shortcomings that hinder mainstream adoption. Mainly, the effort and manpower needed to reduce the error rate in software is still intolerably high.

In our group we are developing fully automatic, yet precise verification tools that can be used to check standard software (like Web browsers/servers or Internet infrastructure software) for security gaps. The basis of our approach is a technique called *Bounded Model Checking*, which is already in common use in the microprocessor design automation community. We apply this method to software, however not on the source-code level, but on a low-level abstract assembler language (LLVM intermediate language[6]). This makes our approach on the one hand independent of the programming language used (like C, C++, Java, or Objective-C), and on the other hand closer to what the machine actually does. Moreover—and in contrast to most previous approaches— we employ a highly precise memory model for our software analysis, which is essential to detect memory errors like buffer overflows with high accuracy. Further techniques utilized in our approach include code simplification by abstract analysis, generation of

---

[3] http://www.informationweek.com/news/internet/showArticle.jhtml?articleID= 199701774.
[4] http://cve.mitre.org/docs/vuln-trends/vuln-trends.pdf.
[5] http://www.blackhat.com.
[6] http://www.llvm.org.

function summaries, and limited employment of user-provided annotations and specifications. Initial experiments with a simple prototype tool on a standard security-related software verification benchmark have already delivered very promising results outperforming existing tools. We expect that with our approach the number of exploitable gaps in current software can be considerably reduced with low to moderate effort. The main cause of cyber attacks—buffer overflows and integer overflows—can thus to a great extent be dispelled.

2.1 Illustrating Example

Buffer overflows, the predominant cause of security gaps, can occur in programs that fail to use appropriate bound checks when accessing memory. An attacker canin such a casewrite data beyond the intended boundaries of a (memory) buffer, thus possibly corrupting control structures in the program. Buffer overflows come in two flavors, as heap buffer overflows and stack buffer overflows. Both of them can be exploited by malicious code, but the details of how exactly this can be accomplished differ. Details can be found, e.g., in Matt Conovers article "w00w00 on Heap Overflows"[7], in Aleph Ones "Smashing the Stack for Fun and Profit"[8], or in the Web tutorial "How to write Buffer Overflows"[9].

```
void foo(char *a) {
  char b[BUFSZ], *p;

  // copy string a to buffer b for(p = b; *a; a++, p++)
  *p = *a;

  // manipulate string in buffer b .
  ...
}
```

Fig. 1. Example of a C function that can cause a stack buffer overflow.

Figure 1 shows an example of a piece of C code which is unsafe: Function `foo` copies input string `a` to a local array `b` of constant size `BUFSZ` (which is placed on the stack). However, it does not check whether the input string fits into the local array. Passing a string longer than `BUFSZ` to function `foo` thus causes a stack buffer overflow, which can be exploited by preparing a specially crafted input string that is passed to the function.

---

[7] http://www.w00w00.org/files/articles/heaptut.txt.
[8] http://insecure.org/stf/smashstack.html.
[9] http://insecure.org/stf/mudge_buffer_overflow_tutorial.html.

3 State of the Art

Due to the importance of the buffer overflow problem, many solutions have been brought up to cope with it. Silberman and Johnson [8] discuss several techniques to prevent buffer overflows and compare tools implementing these techniques. They roughly classify them as either "kernel-enforced protection" or "compiler-enforced protection". Kernel-enforced protection methods include hardware-supported restrictions to write to certain regions of memory (like the NX-bit present on many recent CPUs) and address space layout randomization (as, e.g., implemented in Windows Vista). Compiler-enforced protections take place during translation of the programs source code to machine language. Special precautions are taken, mainly to prevent the modification of return values placed on the stack (by so-called *Stack Canaries*). However, all these techniques have their limitations and can be circumvented, as is demonstrated by Silberman and Johnson. They conclude that "(...) attackers are still one step ahead with methods available to defeat almost every protection mechanism available."

Another possibility is to use special program libraries that perform bounds checks at run-time. Such safe libraries include "The Better String Library,"[10] Vstr[11], and Erwin[12]. However, the efficacy of these libraries for the purpose of reducing buffer overflows is disputable; it requires modifications to the program on a per function call basis, which is cumbersome, and it is often claimed that the time to modify the function calls can also be used to manually add safety guards. Moreover, the performance of the modified program can be drastically diminished. Thus, these librariesalthough helpfulare not widely employed.

Another large class of methods to avoid security breaches is based on formal methods like static analysis, interactive verification, or model checking. These methods do not intervene at run-time of the program, but perform a security analysis on the source code in advance (thus the term static). The following list gives a short overview of existing methods:

Static Analysis: Static analysis tools (e.g., [6, 11, 12]) analyze a program on the source code level, often by overapproximating its behavior and computing possible sets of variable values (e.g., intervals) at each program location (data-flow analysis). However, many of these tools suffer from poor precision in that they either report many false errors (*false positives*) or miss errors (*false negatives*). The former requires considerable manual effort to check error reports, which is often not accepted by programmers.

Interactive Verification: Interactive program verification, like implemented, e.g., in the KeY system [2], requires the programmer to add specification annotations as well as assertions to his program and conduct correctness proofs for the assertions manually, but with assistance from the system (such as tactics). The proofs are made in expressive logics like first-order dynamic logic in case of the KeY system. This is an advantage as high level properties involving complex data structures can be analyzed, but also possesses the drawback of requiring substantial user interaction.

---

[10] http://bstring.sourceforge.net.

[11] http://www.and.org/vstr.

[12] http://www.theiling.de/projects/erwin.html.

Model Checking: Software model checking (SMC) is a technique that has achieved success in finding errors in critical systems [10] or proving their absence [1]. Model checking typically has the advantage of high precision in that the number of false error reports is very low or even zero. But often the programs are too complex to be examined by model checkers. Software model checkers are either based on abstraction refinement, like, e.g., BLAST [7] or SatAbs [4], or on bounded model checking (e.g., CBMC [3]). Whereas the first approach is (at least in theory) sound and complete (i.e. it neither gives false error reports nor misses any errors), the latter is not. It is nevertheless useful, as it can find many errors faster than abstraction refinement tools, and thus makes a valuable debugging tool.

Abstraction Refinement: This technique typically starts with an abstraction (approximation) of the program obtained, e.g., by replacing an integer variable x with a Boolean predicate, e.g. $x > 0$ (*predicate abstraction*). The program is then analyzed on the abstracted level and gradually refined by introducing additional predicates (e.g. $x < 5$), until the property has been proven or a counterexample has been found.

Bounded Model Checking: Bounded model checking considers finite paths in software source code and checks properties of these finite paths. The paths are obtained by unrolling loops and unwinding recursions up to a fixed bound (this also implies a fixed amount of memory that can be accessed by the program). This program is then converted into bit-vector equations (bit-vectors represent, e.g., machine integers) expressing the semantics of the program. Finally these equations are converted into propositional logic formulas (e.g., by replacing an integer multiplication by the hardware circuit that computes this multiplication) and passed to a SAT solver. Properties to be checked are either specified using assert and assume statements (Hoare style) or are already built-in (like integer overflows or array bounds checks).

Combinations of these methods are also possible. ESC/Java [5], for example, combines static analysis with annotations like in interactive verification.

4 Software Bounded Model Checking

4.1 Outline

Our approach for verification of security properties is based on bounded model checking, as initial experiments have shown the potential of this method. The overall structure of our verification approach is shown in Figure 2. Starting with the program under examination (written in C, C++ or another language), this is first translated to an abstract assembler intermediate language by a compiler front-end. Our verification then starts at this level by performing a logical encoding resulting in another, more logic-oriented intermediate constraint language (using bit-vector logic with arrays and uninterpreted functions). This is then either converted to a propositional logic formula by a technique called bit-blasting or directly passed to an SMT solver for the logic of bit-vectors plus arrays.

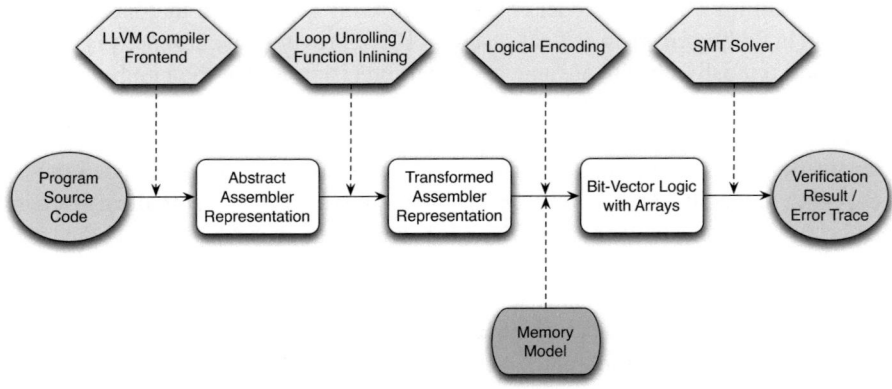

Fig. 2. Schematics of our Verification Approach.

In contrast to existing approaches (as implemented, e.g., in CBMC [3]), we use a variety of different techniques for increasing the degree of automation and to make it scale better to larger software. These new techniques are:

1. Verification is performed not on the software source code level, but on an abstract assembler-like intermediate language. This approach has a number of advantages over directly verifying source code:

    (a) It avoids the complicated semantics of programming languages like C or C++, which makes implementing verification tools much harder. Low-level assembler code has a much simpler semantics and fewer syntactic constructs. Using abstract assembler produced by a compiler front end also makes our verification tools programming language independent: all languages supported by the compiler front end are directly accessible to the verification tool.

    (b) The simple load-store semantics of the intermediate language we are planning to use in this project requires less expressive logics for formalization.

    (c) We get source code optimizations for free, as they are already implemented in the compiler front end. Advances in compiler technology are immediately accessible to our tools, without a need to modify them.

    (d) Transformation to static single assignment (SSA) form, which is required for the translation to Boolean logic, comes for free, as it is already implemented in the compiler front-end.

2. Use of a highly precise memory model. Software bounded model checking tools often use inaccurate memory models. The static checker Calysto [13], which is also based on bounded model checking, e.g., handles pointer arithmetic in an unsound manner. But to identify memory access errors like buffer overflows, high accuracy in modeling memory access is mandatory.

3. Aggressive optimization on all levels of the verification chain. To make our method more scalable, we want to apply optimizations on different levels:

(a) The compiler front-end already implements compiler-based optimizations like constant propagation. We may also implement additional techniques like partial evaluation as add-ons to the (open-source) compiler front-end.

(b) On the intermediate constraint language further optimizations are possible, like guard simplification, dependency analysis and slicing. We already experimented with optimizations of this kind with CBMC and achieved dramatic improvements (factors in the order of 10 to 100 in problem solving time).

(c) Different forms of conversion to CNF as well as new problem-specific heuristics used in the SAT solver allow further optimization. First experiments with a technique similar to that proposed by Marques-Silva and Lynce [14] showed great potential.

4. On-demand lemma generation. This is a technique that is already successfully applied in Satisfiability-Modulo-Theory (SMT) solvers [15]. In our approach, it can be used on the bit-vector logic level, as proposed in the literature. However, there is another way to make use of these on-demand lemmas, namely in

5. Generation of function and loop summaries in a logic with quantifiers. Using this technique scalability is to be improved. The user can specify loop invariants and function summaries in a more expressive logic (similar to JML annotations). These user-specified annotations are then used as lemmas on demand.

6. Iterative refinement of the call-graph. If the software becomes too large, modular techniques have to be applied. In work on verification of drivers in the Linux kernel, we already experimented with an iterative refinement of the program context that is considered during verification: starting with only one function, which is search for errors, the context is gradually extended taking the call-graph into account.

5 Challenges and Research Outlook

Software verification is on its way from a purely academic research tool to being applied in real software projects.

Even today's tools are able to detect many (low-level) errors in programs. However, the effort needed to apply them, is still considerable. Future work thus includes:

- Allow for full coverage of all language constructs occurring in high-level programming languages (like C++/Java).
- Increase applicability by using formalisms as simple as possible for the user of a verification tool.
- Increase scalability by using new optimization techniques and new algorithms (e.g. for handling loops, better SMT performance).
- Better feedback to the user on where and under which circumstances an error occurs.

In total, we expect that the combination of all these techniques has the potential for a huge leap forward towards complete elimination of security-critical faults in programs.

6 The Research Group "Verification meets Algorithm Engineering"

The research group "Verification meets Algorithm Engineering" currently consists of five scientific members. Our work is focused on software verification, ranging from fundamental research (e.g. on logical decision procedures), over verification algorithm development, to applications. The research plan for our group can be described as *vertically integrated research*, as we cover all topics from basic research to application.

In particular, our group members perform research in the following areas:

Fig. 3. The research group "Verification meets Algorithm Engineering". From left to right: F. Merz, O. Tveretina, C. Sinz, S. Falke.

1. *Olga Tveretina*: Comparative complexity analysis of propositional logic decision procedures (like SAT solvers or BDDs); decidable fragments of hybrid systems.
2. *Christian Vetter*: New algorithms for the propositional logic satisfiability (SAT) problem.
3. *Stephan Falke* and *Florian Merz*: Low-level software bounded model checking, including development of the tool LLBMC, a state-of-the-art software bounded model checker based on the compiler front-end LLVM.

References

1. T. Ball and S. Rajamani. The SLAM toolkit. In *Proc. CAV01*, pages 260–264, 2001.
2. B. Beckert, R. Hähnle, and P.H. Schmitt. *Verification of Object-Oriented Software: The KeY Approach*. Number 4334 in LNCS. Springer-Verlag, 2007.
3. E. Clarke, D. Kröning, and F. Lerda. A tool for checking ANSI-C programs. In *Proc. TACAS04*, pages 168–176, 2004.
4. E. Clarke, D. Krning, N. Sharygina, and K. Yorav. SATABS: SAT-based predicate abstraction for ANSI-C. In *Proc. TACAS'05*, pages 570–574, 2005.
5. C. Flanagan, K. Rustan, M. Leino, M. Lillibridge, G. Nelson, J.B. Saxe, and R. Stata. Extended static checking for Java. In *Proc. PLDI'02*, pages 234–245, 2002.
6. B. Hacket, M. Das, D. Wang, and Z. Yang. Modular checking for buffer overflows in the large. In *Proc. ICSE'06*, pages 232–241, 2006.
7. T. Henzinger, R. Jhala, R. Majumdar, and G. Sutre. Lazy abstraction. In *Proc. POPL'02*, pages 58–70, 2002.
8. P. Silberman and R. Richardson. A comparison of buffer overflow prevention implementations and weaknesses. In *BlackHat Asia Conference*, 2004.

9. Alan M. Turing. Checking a large routine. In *Report of a Conference on High Speed Calculating Machines*, pages 67–69. University Mathematical Laboratory, Cambridge, June 1949.

10. W. Visser, K. Havelund, G. Brat, S. Park, and F. Lerda. Model checking programs. *J. Automated Software Engineering*, 10(2), April 2003.

11. D. Wagner, J.S. Foster, E.A. Brewer, and A. Aiken. A first step towards automated detection of buffer overrun vulnerabilities. In *Proc. NDSS'00*, pages 3–17, 2000.

12. Y. Xie, A. Chou, and D.R. Engler. ARCHER: Using symbolic, path-sensitive analysis to detect memory access errors. In *Proc. ESEC/FSE-11*, pages 327–336, 2003.

Data Privacy in Novel
Ubiquitous Computing Applications

Erik Buchmann

Karlsruhe Institute of Technology, Germany
buchmann@kit.edu

Abstract. In the last years, newspapers have frequently reported privacy violations. Enterprises, data privacy authorities and individuals concerned are overstrained with the number of services acquiring and processing personal data on the web, and with the daunting number of regulations. It can be expected that privacy threats become more and more serious in the future, when novel information technologies enter the mass-market. This paper introduces in the long-term vision and the research projects of the young investigator group "Privacy Awareness in Information Systems and its Implications on Society". The research group focuses on privacy in scenarios where information technology is ubiquitously present, e.g., as RFID labels in the supermarket, sensor networks in public spaces or novel Internet applications that are part of the everyday life of many persons.

1 Introduction

We are about to gain a new understanding of privateness, with unpredictable consequences for the society. It has never been as simple as today to collect large volumes of personal data, and it has never been so hard for the individuals concerned to trace the whereabouts of all kinds of personal information. Advances in the areas of ubiquitous computing [27] are about to bridge the gap between the online and offline world, and challenge data privacy significantly. Cellphones with Internet connectivity are used by large shares of society, RFID [33] labels are about to replace the barcodes in the supermarkets, and many sensor networks [20] applications have been proposed by industry and research. The smart grid (a.k.a. Internet of Energy) is about to carry information devices like smart meters into the homes of every energy consumer.

The Internet connects all these devices, and allows to collect, manage, store and combine personal information from many different sources. In consequence, the personal and factual living conditions of more and more people are represented on the Internet. This includes the social network of friends, classmates or colleagues, personal preferences, trajectories, personal possessions etc. A prominent example is Google Latitude[1]. It displays the movement of the cellphones of persons which have subscribed the service, and allows certain individuals to observe the current locations of friends. The amount of personal information available on the Internet is huge, and it is increasing day by day. The social impact of these developments is problematic. The more personal information visible on the Internet, the larger are the risks for identity theft, account

---

[1] http://www.google.com/latitude

79

fraud, stalking or bullying. If we do not find practical approaches for privacy protection, it might become as simple as using a search engine to assemble comprehensive personality profiles of many persons. In this paper we describe the current and future work of our young investigator group "Privacy Awareness in Information Systems and its Implications on Society". In particular, we briefly describe recent technologies with an impact on data privacy, present existing privacy protection approaches, and explain why such approaches are inefficient. We introduce our long-term vision of novel collaborative data privacy protection approaches, and we discuss why such approaches can raise the use and efficiency of privacy enhancing technologies.

2   Recent Technologies with an Impact on Privacy

In this section, we introduce ubiquitous computing technologies that threaten the privacy of their users. A **sensor network** [22] consists of many sensor nodes equipped with sensing devices, radio transmitters and limited computational resources. By using self-organization technologies for sensing and network formation, sensor networks fulfill complex measurement tasks in the fields of surveillance, border control or facility monitoring. **Radio Frequency Identification** (RFID) assigns a globally unique identification number to physical objects for applications like object tracking or stock management [14]. The objects are labeled with a RFID tag containing a radio transmitter as well as limited computing and storage capabilities. The tags can be read over a distance without requiring a straight line of sight. One of the most prominent RFID applications is to replace barcode-based processes, in particular at the points of sale of retailers [19]. **Smart devices**, e.g., cellphones with Internet connectivity, smart electricity meters that are part of future power grids, or medical appliances can monitor the behavior of their users around the clock. Some devices, in particular cellphones, are highly integrated into the everyday life of many persons. As a cross-cutting service, the **Internet** enables a broad variety of devices and services to interact in order to drive highly personal, interconnected applications. On the Internet, privacy-sensitive information can be gathered by using cookies, iframes, web-bugs, affiliation programs, services that require a personal login etc. The situation is expected to become even more unclear in the future [21].

The technologies described have a large impact on privacy, for four reasons:

- They bridge the gap between the online and the offline world. Thus, the situation is not as simple as switching off the computer to leave data privacy issues behind.
- The technologies use networked devices to collect, transfer and process personal data in the background and without the assistance and the knowledge of the individual concerned. Thus, it is virtually impossible for each individual to keep track of all service providers which have her personal data.
- As the level of detail of the collected data is comprehensive, and personal data from multiple sources can be easily linked, the potential of any misuse is huge.
- The applications outlined yield a clear benefit for their users. Thus, it is not an option to strictly avoid their use.

3 Data Privacy Approaches

Current solutions for data privacy divide into (1) legal norms and regulations, (2) technical mechanisms and (3) other approaches.

Laws and Regulations. Throughout the European Union, directives establish data privacy as a fundamental human right [18] and harmonize the data privacy law among all EU members. The debates on transposing these directives into national law show that regulatory approaches have fundamental limitations. First, the legislator cannot predict new technologies. This involves periods of time without legal certainty, until regulations have been adopted for new privacy threats. Second, the regulatory approach often results in a daunting number of norms that is unmanageable both for the persons concerned and for the data collectors. Third, it is challenging to enforce data privacy regulations in scenarios where the collection and processing of private data is *intransparent* to the individuals concerned [26]. Furthermore, the resources of the supervisory authorities of data privacy law are limited, while the number of data-collection activities, by a very large number of organizations, is daunting. Thus, the regulatory approach is often ineffective in ensuring data privacy. We have investigated [8] a representative set of 100 large service providers which are subject to German legislation, and we have found out that only 5 of 100 providers comply with current legislation.

Technical Mechanisms. The number of privacy enhancing technologies available is large. Nevertheless, existing technical mechanisms cannot ensure data privacy for the majority of people, for various reasons. For example, P3P-enabled web servers [16] inform the web browser of the user about the privacy policy of the service provider, and let the browser reject cookies which pose a privacy threat according to the user preferences. But understanding the impact of cookies on privacy and therefore setting the preferences accordingly requires a thorough understanding of the Internet protocols. Finally, P3P cannot express all details required from EU privacy regulations, and addresses only a tiny fraction of privacy threats on the Internet (cf. [17]). Other technical mechanisms face similar problems. In particular, all technical privacy-related approaches we are aware of are *technology-centered, isolated* implementations and require a thorough understanding of the technology. For example, an entry 'X-No-Archive: Yes' in the header of Usenet messages prevents them from being filed. But it is hard to explain to persons without a technical background how to make use of such features. We expect that the situation will become worse with more sophisticated technology. This does not mean that it is not important to develop such mechanisms. The finding simply indicates that it cannot be left to the individual to use a large number of specific privacy techniques efficiently.

Other Mechanisms. Considering that both legal and technical mechanisms are not sufficient to ensure data privacy, recent political debates suggest the legislator to focus on self-regulation, education and training [15]. Privacy seals are one approach for self-regulation. They certify that service providers follow specific privacy guidelines [1]. Thus, privacy seals signalize trust in the data-handling practices of the provider audited. However, as long as the prerequisites to obtain a seal are unclear for the most of the public, the significance of privacy seals is limited.

4 Collaborative Privacy Mechanisms

Intuitively speaking, we assume that people are neither interested in going through law-suits nor in implementing technical mechanisms to enforce privacy. Instead of bothering with the details of technologies and regulations, the individuals concerned simply want to know: *"Can I trust a certain service provider to handle my personal information compliant with regulations and according to my preferences?"*. Since existing research does not directly address this demand, it is necessary to investigate new issues and directions for future research and development. Our vision is to develop privacy mechanisms that allow a community of users to collaboratively identify privacy violations, and to share knowledge about violations with others. To bring this vision to life, we have researched three areas: (1) basis technologies needed to realize novel ubiquitous computing approaches, (2) how the society currently handles data privacy protection and (3) privacy mechanisms for current and novel information systems.

Basis Technologies RFID technology will gain a large influence on society. We have investigated how to integrate RFID into enterprises. This includes the estimation of the number [11] and position [12] of RFID tags from unreliable data sources, and the handling of large data sets [13] that are typical for RFID. We have also researched query processing in sensor networks. In particular, we were interested in the optimization of join queries [30, 32, 29] needed to analyze data from multiple sources, and the handling of non-selective queries [31]. Furthermore, we have developed a probabilistic approach to efficiently disseminate queries into sensor networks [2, 3].

Privacy Studies We have investigated if Internet users are able to manage their privacy, given the privacy mechanisms and privacy laws currently available, and we have found that this is not the case: First, it is often intransparent how data collectors manage personal information, and the use of privacy mechanisms requires much awareness from the user [6]. Second, many privacy laws are badly enforced [8]. To identify the scope of privacy needs in novel applications, we have conducted a number of user studies that considered collaborative search engines [5, 7] and location-based services [9]. Our findings indicate that users are interested in sophisticated privacy mechanisms, but fail to use mechanisms properly that are too complicated or require too much attention.

Privacy Mechanisms We have developed a number of privacy mechanisms for current and future information systems, and we have tested them on the Internet. Primo [10] uses face recognition to find photos that have been published without the consent of the persons on the photo. Another approach targets at privacy-aware folksonomies [25]. Folksonomies are one of the most popular Web 2.0 technologies. They allow a community of users to collaboratively annotate digital resources. The annotations might reveal the interests and habits of the users. Our approach encrypts and partitions data so that neither the folksonomy operator nor unauthorized other parties are able learn private information. Finally, our Privacy 2.0 framework [4, 24] allows a community of users to annotate privacy violations and to share those information with others. In order to provide an example for our current work, we now describe Privacy 2.0 in more detail.

4.1 Privacy 2.0

The Privacy 2.0 framework [4] is a holistic approach, designed to cover a wide range of privacy threats. It allows a community of users to intuitively share knowledge about privacy threats. Privacy 2.0 allows to annotate URLs on the Internet, geographical positions obtained from a GPS device or RFID-tagged items read via near field communication with privacy-related tags. The framework provides a warning if a user approaches a site that collects personal information against her preferences. Privacy 2.0 cannot provide absolute guarantees. However, we think that annotations from many individuals would correctly represent privacy issues that are important for large shares of society.

Fig. 1. Overview of the Privacy2.0 Framework

The core component of our framework (Figure 1) is the **PrivacyTagger**, a user-managed taxonomy of data privacy issues. It stores tuples of the form (*privacy threat, user pseudonym, label*). For example, one could tag a geographical position with the labels "video", "surveillance" and "no privacy policy". The **TagMiner** tries to identify labels with the same meaning. For example, the labels "worse policy" and "spammer" provide the same negative assessment. To find out if privacy threats identified by one user are relevant for another one, the **PreferenceMatcher** computes the similarity of two users, based on the tagged objects and the tags they have created. The **ThreatTaxonomy** determines similar services, locations and objects. Finally, the **IncentivesManager** motivates the users to create useful and reliable labels, e.g., by providing better service for dependable users. We have evaluated Privacy 2.0 by means of a user study [24] on a prototypical implementation. The study acknowledges that the concept of Privacy 2.0 is applicable to real-world privacy threats on the Internet.

5 Future Research Directions

Besides continuing our work on ongoing research projects, we plan to focus our future research efforts on smart grid scenarios. The smart grid combines sensor networks, smart devices, RFID and Internet technology to an "Internet of Energy" [23]. It is intended to realize an intelligent, decentralized distribution and transmission network for electricity that saves energy by managing energy sources and energy consumer efficiently. Amongst others, the smart grid strives to optimize energy consumers such as domestic refrigerators, washing machines or the chargers of electric cars as well as energy sources like photovoltaic solar power plants on the roofs of private buildings. Therefore, the smart grid realizes a number of services, e.g., building virtual power consumers from a large number of dishwashers, using the batteries of electric cars as storage power stations or providing automated energy consultations. These services require energy data with a high resolution. For example, the smart meters that are mandatory for each new building in Germany since 1/1/2010 send via WLAN or powerline communication every 15 minutes precise energy consumption data to the energy provider. Such information might reveal personal information [28], e.g., if a person wants to travel by her electric car, or if she uses her TV set late at night. Our vision is to develop privacy techniques for the smart grid that allow the services envisioned without affecting the privacy of the individuals concerned. Furthermore, we strive for collaborative approaches that enable a community of users to share information about energy providers which (do not) handle personal information with care.

6 Conclusion

The integration of current and future information technologies in the everyday life will shape the society of the future not only because of its benefits, but also due to significant new challenges with regard to data privacy. Current solutions for data privacy require time and effort from the user. In the presence of many networked devices to collect, transfer and process personal data, these solutions cannot ensure privacy.

Our objective is to investigate privacy mechanisms that allow services without revealing personal information, and to deploy collaborative technologies that support individuals in protecting their privacy by making use of the knowledge of a large user community. To this end, we have studied the current situation of data privacy protection in novel information systems, and we have developed a number of privacy approaches, e.g., Primo, Privacy 2.0 or a privacy-aware folksonomy system. In the future, we plan to focus our research on the privacy issues that are part of the smart grid.

7 Short CV

Erik Buchmann was born in Magdeburg, Germany in 1976. He received his Diploma (M.Sc.) in Business Informatics from the Otto-von-Guericke-University of Magdeburg, Germany in 2002. In 2006, he earned his Ph.D. in Computer Science (summa cum laude) from the same university. Since September 2006, Erik Buchmann is a research associate of the IPD, Universitt Karlsruhe (TH). By 2007, he became head of the Young

Investigator Group "Privacy Awareness in Information Systems and its Implications on Society". His research interests include wireless sensor networks, self-organizing embedded systems and the impact of all kinds of ubiquitous systems on society.

References

1. Beatty, P., Reay, I., Dick, S., Miller, J.: P3P Adoption on E-Commerce Web sites: A Survey and Analysis. IEEE Internet Computing (IC) 11(2), 65–71 (2007)
2. Benenson, Z., Bestehorn, M., Buchmann, E., Freiling, F., Jawurek, M.: Query Dissemination with Predictable Reachability and Energy Usage in Sensor Networks. In: Proceedings of the 7th International Conference on AD-HOC Networks and Wireless (ADHOC-NOW'08) (Sep 2008)
3. Bestehorn, M., Benenson, Z., Buchmann, E., Jawurek, M., Böhm, K., Freiling, F.: Query Dissemination in Sensor Networks - Predicting Reachability and Energy Consumption. In: Ad Hoc and Sensor Wireless Networks (2009)
4. Buchmann, E., Böhm, K., Raabe, O.: Privacy2.0: Towards Collaborative Data-Privacy Protection. In: Proceedings of the 2nd Joint iTrust and PST Conferences on Privacy, Trust Management and Security (IFIPTM'08) (Jun 2008)
5. Burghardt, T., Buchmann, E., Böhm, K.: Discovering the Scope of Privacy Needs in Collaborative Search. In: Proceedings of the IEEE/WIC/ACM International Conference on Web Intelligence (WI'08) (Dec 2008)
6. Burghardt, T., Buchmann, E., Böhm, K.: Why Do Privacy-Enhancement Mechanisms Fail, After All? In: Proceedings of the International Workshop on Web 2.0 Trust (W2Trust'08) (Jun 2008)
7. Burghardt, T., Buchmann, E., Böhm, K., Clifton, C.: Collaborative Search And User Privacy: How Can They Be Reconciled? In: Proceedings of the 4th International Conference on Collaborative Computing (CollaborateCom'08) (Nov 2008)
8. Burghardt, T., Buchmann, E., Böhm, K., Kühling, J., Sivridis, A.: A Study on the Lack of Enforcement of Data Protection Acts. In: Proceedings of the 3rd International Conference on e-Democracy (Sep 2009)
9. Burghardt, T., Buchmann, E., Müller, J., Böhm, K.: Understanding User Preferences and Awareness: Privacy Mechanisms in Location-Based Services. In: Proceedings of the 17th International Conference on Cooperative Information Systems (CoopIS'09) (Nov 2009)
10. Burghardt, T., Walter, A., Buchmann, E., Böhm, K.: PRIMO - Towards Privacy Aware Image Sharing. In: Proceedings of the 2nd Workshop on Collective Intelligence in Semantic Web and Social Networks (CISWSN'08) (Dec 2008)
11. Chaves, L.W.F., Buchmann, E., Böhm, K.: TagMark: Reliable Estimations of RFID Tags for Business Processes. In: Proceedings of the 14th Conference on Knowledge Discovery and Data Mining (KDD'08) (Aug 2008)
12. Chaves, L.W.F., Buchmann, E., Böhm, K.: RPCV: RFID Planogram Compliance Verification. In: Proceedings of the International Conference on Extending Database Technologies (EDBT'10) (Mar 2010)
13. Chaves, L.W.F., Buchmann, E., Hüske, F., Böhm, K.: Optimizing Complex, Distributed Database Transactions using Materialized Views. In: Proceedings of the International Conference on Extending Database Technologies (EDBT'09) (Mar 2009)
14. Chawathe, S.S., et al.: Managing RFID Data. In: Proceedings of the 30st International Conference on Very Large Data Bases (VLDB'04) (2004)
15. Concil of the European Union: European Policy Outlook RFID (draft version). Working document for the expert conference "RFID: Towards the Internet of Things" (Jun 2007)

16. Cranor, L., et al.: The Platform for Privacy Preferences 1.0 (p3p1.0). W3C Recommendation, Available at http://www.w3.org/TR/P3P/ (Apr 2002)
17. Electronic Privacy Information Center: Pretty Poor Privacy: An Assessment of P3P and Internet Privacy. Available at http://www.epic.org/reports/prettypoorprivacy.html (2000)
18. European Parliament and the Council of the European Union: Directive 95/46/EC on the protection of individuals with regard to the processing of personal data and on the free movement of such data. Official Journal L 281, 11/23/1995, p.31. (1995)
19. Gaukler, G.M., Seifert, R.W., Hausman, W.H.: Item-Level RFID in the Retail Supply Chain. Production and Operations Management 16, 65–76 (2007)
20. Gehrke, J., Madden, S.: Query Processing in Sensor Networks. IEEE Pervasive Computing 03(1), 46–55 (2004)
21. Gorbis, M., Pescovitz, D.: Bursting Tech Bubbles Before They Balloon. In: IEEE Spektrum (2006)
22. Haenselmann, T.: An FDL'ed Textbook on Sensor Networks. Published under GNU FDL at http://www.informatik.uni-mannheim.de/˜haensel/sn_book (2005)
23. Hassan, R., Radman, G.: Survey on Smart Grid. In: Proceedings of the IEEE SoutheastCon 2010 (Mar 2010)
24. Heidinger, C., Buchmann, E., Böhm, K.: Collaborative Data Privacy for the Web. In: Proceedings of the 3rd International Workshop on Privacy and Anonymity in the Information Society (PAIS'20) (Mar 2010)
25. Heidinger, C., Buchmann, E., Huber, M., Böhm, K., Müller-Quade, J.: Privacy-Aware Folksonomies. In: Proceedings of the 14th European Conference on Research and Advanced Technology for Digital Libraries (ECDL'10) (Sep 2010)
26. Klver, L., et al.: ICT and Privacy in Europe – A Report on Different Aspects of Privacy Based on Studies Made by EPTA Members in 7 European Countries. Available at DOI: http://dx.doi.org/10.1553/ITA-pb-a44s (Oct 2006)
27. Langheinrich, M.: A Privacy Awareness System for Ubiquitous Computing Environments. In: Proceedings of the 4th International Conference on Ubiquitous Computing (UbiComp'02). pp. 237–245 (2002)
28. McDaniel, P., McLaughlin, S.: Security and Privacy Challenges in the Smart Grid. IEEE Security and Privacy 7, 75–77 (2009)
29. Stern, M., Böhm, K., Buchmann, E.: Processing Continuous Join Queries in Sensor Networks: a Filtering Approach. In: Proceedings of the 29th International Conference on Management of Data (SIGMOD'10) (Jun 2010)
30. Stern, M., Buchmann, E., Böhm, K.: Where in the Sensor Network Should the Join Be Computed, After All? In: Proceedings of the First Ubiquitous Knowledge Discovery Workshop (UKD'08) (Sep 2008)
31. Stern, M., Buchmann, E., Böhm, K.: A Wavelet Transform for Efficient Consolidation of Sensor Relations with Quality Guarantees. In: Proceedings of the 35th International Conference on Very Large Data Bases (VLDB'09) (Aug 2009)
32. Stern, M., Buchmann, E., Böhm, K.: Towards Efficient Processing of General-Purpose Joins in Sensor Networks. In: Proceedings of the 25th International Conference on Data Engineering (ICDE'09) (Mar 2009)
33. Wang, F., Liu, P.: Temporal Management of RFID Data. In: Proceedings of the 31st International Conference on Very Large Data Bases (VLDB'05). pp. 1128–1139 (2005)

The what, why, and how
of provably secure encryption

Dennis Hofheinz

Institut für Kryptographie und Sicherheit
Fakultät für Informatik
Karlsruher Institut für Technologie
http://www.iks.kit.edu/hofheinz/
Dennis.Hofheinz@kit.edu

1 Introduction

Did you use webmail today? Or did you recently log into your, say, Facebook or E-Bay account? If so, then you will probably have used a connection that was secured (through the `https` protocol) with digital encryption. This means that, e.g., your emails have been encrypted by your webmail service prior to transmission. This was done to ensure that no "man in the middle" between you and your email provider can read your emails as you view them.

Our research group at the Institut für Kryptographie und Sicherheit at the KIT deals with the design and analysis of encryption schemes suitable for real-life applications as above. In this article, we will showcase recent and ongoing research projects.

Secret key encryption. Encryption schemes can be divided into two categories: public key encryption schemes, and private key encryption schemes. Private key encryption schemes are well-known for centuries: to encrypt a message, a secret key K is required; the same secret key K is needed to decrypt the ciphertext. Early examples of this type of encryption are the scheme that Julius Caesar used for securely communicating messages to his troops ("Caesar cipher"), or the scheme used to secure the Moscow-Washington hotline ("one-time pad").

Public key encryption. A practical drawback of private key encryption schemes like these is that a common key between the communicating peers is required. Usually, a prior physical meeting is necessary to exchange such a key. Public key encryption, on the other hand, does not require a shared secret key. In a public key encryption scheme, the keys required for encryption and decryption are different. Namely, the encryption key is called *public* key, whereas the key necessary for decryption is called *secret* key. In particular, it is not necessary to keep the public key in any way hidden; it can indeed be publicized. In fact, anybody who wants to talk to, say, Alice, can look up Alice's public key in a public directory and encrypt his messages under Alice's public key. The security properties of a public key encryption scheme guarantee that only Alice can decrypt a message encrypted that way.

Example: RSA encryption. Public key encryption is relatively new concept. One of the earliest examples of public key encryption schemes is the RSA scheme [12], named after its inventors Rivest, Shamir, and Adleman. In that scheme, the public key pk consists of a large composite number $N = PQ$ for primes P and Q, and an integer e. The encryption of a message $M \in \mathbb{Z}_N$ is defined as $\mathsf{Enc}(pk, M) = M^e \bmod N$. The secret key sk in the RSA scheme is an integer d satisfying $ed \equiv 1 \bmod (P-1)(Q-1)$, such that $(M^e)^d \equiv M \bmod N$. Hence, the decryption of a ciphertext C is simply $\mathsf{Dec}(sk, C) = C^d \bmod N$. (We will not be concerned here with the exact way N, e, and d are chosen.)

The RSA encryption scheme is extremely simple and intuitive. However, in the presented form, it is unsuitable for any practical usage. Namely, observe that encryption is deterministic (i.e., encryption of the same message always leads to

Public key: $pk = (N, e)$
Secret key: $sk = (N, d)$
Encryption: $\mathsf{Enc}(pk, M) = M^e \bmod N$
Decryption: $\mathsf{Dec}(sk, C) = C^d \bmod N$

Fig. 1. The RSA encryption scheme [12]

the same ciphertext). Hence, any adversary who already knows that the encrypted message is from a small set of possible messages (e.g., $\{\mathtt{yes}, \mathtt{no}\}$) can decrypt without secret key by simply encrypting all message candidates and comparing!

How (not) to overcome a weakness of RSA. It seems intriguing to try to overcome the above weakness of RSA by artificially randomizing the message to be encrypted. That is, instead of encrypting M with RSA, encrypt $M \| R$. Here, $\|$ denotes concatenation of bitstrings, and R is a uniformly random bitstring that is chosen anew upon each encryption. This way, two encryptions of the same message produce different ciphertexts (assuming a suitably long R). Let's call this modified scheme *Randomized RSA*, or just *RRSA*. Amazingly, a variant of the simple RRSA scheme was standardized for internet public key encryption [13]. In particular, for years the Netscape Navigator and Microsoft Internet Explorer browser used essentially RRSA for their encryption of secure internet connections.[1]

Several years later, in 1998, however, Daniel Bleichenbacher discovered that the standardized RRSA variant was vulnerable to a sophisticated attack [4]. His attack used the homomorphic properties of the original RSA scheme (e.g., $\mathsf{Enc}(pk, M_1) \cdot \mathsf{Enc}(pk, M_2) = \mathsf{Enc}(pk, M_1 \cdot M_2)$) that were only partially destroyed by the RRSA random padding and further modifications. Such homomorphic properties can be used to decrypt a given ciphertext by checking if innocent-looking but subtly related ciphertexts can still be decrypted. His attack led to a hasty update of encryption standards and browser libraries. However, to avoid

---

[1] The PKCS standard suggests concrete choices of encryption schemes and key sizes. Of course, an actual encrypted communication session consists of more than only public key encryptions; however, public key encryption forms an integral part of such a session.

another similar fiasco, this time a *provably secure* encryption scheme was standardized. That denotes an encryption scheme for which certain security features (including immunity to a large class of attacks) are mathematically proven.

RSA-OAEP, and why we should not settle for it. For the updated encryption standard, the RSA variant RSA-OAEP [2] (for "RSA Optimal Asymmetric Encryption Padding") was chosen. Up to today, this scheme is still used to secure internet communication sessions. As noted above, RSA-OAEP is accompanied by a mathematical proof that to break its security, it is *necessary* to solve a well-defined mathematical problem.

The problem that is underlying RSA-OAEP's security is called the RSA problem: given (N, e, C) for uniform $C \in \mathbb{Z}_N$, find M with $M^e \equiv C \bmod N$.

Input: (N, e, C) with uniform $C \in \mathbb{Z}_N$
Goal: find M with $M^e \equiv C \bmod N$

Fig. 2. The RSA problem

To break RSA-OAEP, one *must* solve an instance of the RSA problem. There is no shortcut. It should be stressed that by "breaking" an encryption scheme we do not simply mean decrypting a given random ciphertext. A hypothetical attacker A is challenged to only distinguish the encryptions of two messages M_0, M_1 that A himself chose. In the process, A even gets (limited) access to a decryption facility. Hence, by saying that a scheme is secure, we actually mean that any A that is able to distinguish two encryptions of self-chosen messages (even given limited decryption access) can be efficiently transformed into an algorithm that solves the RSA problem.

However, there are two shortcomings of the RSA-OAEP security proof:

- RSA-OAEP's security proof is actually only a heuristic, but no true proof. More specifically, the scheme is only known to be secure in the above sense in the "random oracle model," an idealized model of computation. Even worse, there are indications that no full security proof for RSA-OAEP can be found with standard techniques [11].
- Breaking RSA-OAEP is only "as hard as" solving the RSA problem. However, the RSA problem itself is mathematically not very well-understood. It is still an unsettled question whether the RSA problem is equivalent to the problem of factoring N. (Again, there are indications that this is not the case; i.e., solving the RSA problem may be easier than factoring N.)

Thus, while there is no concrete attack on the RSA-OAEP scheme is known, the scheme's security properties are far from being well-understood.

2 Provably secure encryption schemes

One core research topic in our group is the construction of *provably secure* encryption schemes. By that, we mean encryption schemes whose security can be mathematically proven, without resorting to heuristics as in the case of RSA-OAEP.

Secure encryption from the factorization problem. Concretely, we have devised the first encryption scheme [9] that is provably as hard to break as the factorization problem: given $N = PQ$ for primes P and Q, find P and Q.

Our scheme is only slightly

Input: $N = PQ$ for primes P and Q
Goal: find P and Q

Fig. 3. The factorization problem

less efficient than the current RSA-OAEP standard. However, in stark contrast to RSA-OAEP, our scheme carries a rigorous mathematical proof (without heuristics) that the only way to break our scheme is to solve the factorization problem.

Efficient secure encryption with elliptic curves. While being very attractive from a conceptual perspective, encryption schemes based on the RSA or the factorization problem tend to require large keys. This stems from the fact that current algorithms (e.g., the number field sieve) are able to efficiently factor surprisingly large numbers. Currently, N as in the RSA-OAEP or our scheme from [9] should be chosen of size at least in the order of 2048 bits. Consequently, keys as well as ciphertexts in such schemes occupy several kilobytes of storage; also, encryption and decryption as performed by these schemes quickly become inefficient with larger keys.

An alternative is given by encryption schemes implemented over elliptic curves. In elliptic curve cryptography, computations do not take place modulo a large composite number N, but instead in algebraic groups called "elliptic curves." For such schemes, key and ciphertext sizes can be chosen as low as around 400 bits. Furthermore, encryption and decryption can be implemented much faster than with RSA- or factorization-based schemes.

One of our projects concerns the design and analysis of an efficient and provably secure encryption scheme that can be implemented over elliptic curves. In [8], we devised a scheme that is to date the most efficient provably secure encryption scheme based on elliptic curves. In particular, the scheme is substantially more efficient than the currently standardized RSA-OAEP scheme.

Encryption over lattices. A third example of our work focuses on the possibility of quantum computers. Namely, in case of algorithmic progress, and specifically when sufficiently powerful quantum computers can be built, all currently used encryption technology may be rendered insecure and useless. For instance, there exist concrete algorithmic proposals on how currently used cryptography can be successfully attacked using quantum computers [14]. In this worst-case scenario, cryptographic alternatives need to be available that are in particular not susceptible to quantum attacks.

In [5], we present such an encryption scheme that is based on certain mathematical problems concerning lattices. In particular, we construct the first provably secure encryption schemes that meet the highest current security standard for encryption schemes. Our schemes provide a meaningful alternative even when powerful quantum computers become available.

New design concepts. Crucial to the success of our projects were new design techniques. None of our schemes [8, 9, 5] can be explained in previous design methodologies. For instance, our elliptic curve based scheme [8] is constructed using a new form of hybrid encryption paradigm.[2] Our factorization based scheme [9] melds ideas from pseudorandom number generation and public key encryption techniques. Our lattice based scheme pushes basis generation techniques in lattices further. All of these techniques have since been generalized and generated follow-up work.

3 Encryption with special properties

Another core topic in our research group is the construction of encryption schemes that carry special security properties. These special properties are not implied by standard definitions of security, but become relevant in important use cases.

Example: sensor networks. Consider a large number of tiny devices that are distributed over a large area and periodically send data back to a single receiver. For instance, one could think of sensors that send their measurement results. Imagine that to keep the data hidden from an adversary, the data is encrypted using the public key of the receiver. Suppose now that the adversary is mobile in the sense that it can adaptively corrupt (i.e., open) a small fraction of the devices, and thus open a small fraction of encryptions. Of course, we cannot protect the data that corrupted devices send. But it seems reasonable to expect that data encrypted by uncorrupted devices remains secure (i.e., hidden from the adversary).

Surprisingly, current security notions for public key encryption schemes do *not* guarantee security in this setting. This is so since current notions consider only *static* adversaries that initially decide on who to corrupt.

In [3, 6], we have devised security notions and encryption schemes secure even in the presence of an adaptive adversary. Of course, our schemes carry security proofs. Our schemes use established ("non-committing encryption") as well as only recently discovered methodologies ("lossy encryption").

Example: hibernation. Assume you are hibernating a laptop that uses harddisk encryption. Hibernation stores the current main memory contents on disk. However, if the harddisk is encrypted, then the main memory contains the decryption key in plain. Hence an encryption of the decryption key itself is stored on disk. While a somewhat nonstandard scenario, one should expect that the encryption scheme guarantees security of the so-stored decryption key. However, this is not necessarily the case: standard security notions do not imply security in the presence of key-dependent encryptions. In fact, encryption schemes exist that immediately lose their security once the secret key is encrypted.

---

[2] Hybrid encryption combines the functionality of a public key encryption scheme with the efficiency of a private key encryption scheme.

This situation also arises in other contexts: when trying to prove the applicability of formal methods to cryptographic protocols, encryption schemes that remain secure in the presence of key-dependent messages as above seem necessary. Finally, certain specialized protocols (e.g., for flexibly distributing credentials) require this type of security from an encryption scheme.

Constructing key-dependent message encryption schemes is extremely difficult in the general case [7]. However, we could devise solutions for concrete use cases in [10, 1]. For instance, in [10], we have constructed secure private key schemes that are *stateful* (i.e., the secret key is updated after each encryption). Also, for the case of applying formal methods to cryptographic protocol, we could give a sufficient scheme in [1]. The core idea that we used is that the scheme's complexity depends on the protocol to which it is applied.

4 Conclusion

By now, we know that efficient encryption schemes with mathematically provable security guarantees are not out of reach. However, all standardized and widely deployed schemes carry at best heuristic security guarantees. This is a highly unsatisfying situation: the use of unproven schemes invites cryptographic attacks, as the PKCS fiasco described above demonstrates. We believe the only option is to use provably secure encryption schemes. Thus our mission is to construct even more efficient and more flexible provably secure encryption schemes that are attractive for practitioners.

Short biographical sketch

Dennis Hofheinz was born on February 21, 1979 in Siegen. He studied computer science at the Universität Karlsruhe (TH) from 1998 until 2002. From 2002 to 2005, he was a research assistant at the Institut für Algorithmen und Kognitive Systeme (IAKS) at the Universität Karlsruhe (TH), working in the field of cryptographic protocols. In May 2005, he obtained his doctoral degree under the supervision of Prof. Dr. Thomas Beth.

From 2005 until 2009, he worked as a postdoctoral researcher at the Centrum Wiskunde en Informatica (CWI) in Amsterdam, in the group of Prof. Dr. Ronald Cramer. Since December 2009, he is Juniorprofessor at the Institut für Kryptographie und Sicherheit (IKS) at the Karlsruher Institut für Technologie. He and his group are interested in all areas of theoretic cryptography, but in particular in the design and analysis of provably secure encryption schemes and cryptographic protocols.

References

[1] Boaz Barak, Iftach Haitner, Dennis Hofheinz, and Yuval Ishai. Bounded key-dependent message security. In Henri Gilbert, editor, *Advances in Cryptology,*

Proceedings of EUROCRYPT 2010, Lecture Notes in Computer Science. Springer-Verlag, 2010. To be published.

[2] Mihir Bellare and Phillip Rogaway. Optimal asymmetric encryption—how to encrypt with RSA. In Alfredo de Santis, editor, *Advances in Cryptology, Proceedings of EUROCRYPT '94*, number 950 in Lecture Notes in Computer Science, pages 92–111. Springer-Verlag, 1995.

[3] Mihir Bellare, Dennis Hofheinz, and Scott Yilek. Possibility and impossibility results for encryption and commitment secure under selective opening. In Antoine Joux, editor, *Advances in Cryptology, Proceedings of EUROCRYPT 2009*, number 5479 in Lecture Notes in Computer Science, pages 1–35. Springer-Verlag, 2009.

[4] Daniel Bleichenbacher. Chosen ciphertext attacks against protocols based on the RSA encryption standard PKCS #1. In Hugo Krawczyk, editor, *Advances in Cryptology, Proceedings of CRYPTO '98*, number 1462 in Lecture Notes in Computer Science, pages 1–12. Springer-Verlag, 1998.

[5] David Cash, Dennis Hofheinz, Eike Kiltz, and Chris Peikert. Bonsai trees, or how to delegate a lattice basis. In Henri Gilbert, editor, *Advances in Cryptology, Proceedings of EUROCRYPT 2010*, Lecture Notes in Computer Science. Springer-Verlag, 2010. To be published.

[6] Serge Fehr, Dennis Hofheinz, Eike Kiltz, and Hoeteck Wee. Encryption schemes secure against chosen-ciphertext selective opening attacks. In Henri Gilbert, editor, *Advances in Cryptology, Proceedings of EUROCRYPT 2010*, Lecture Notes in Computer Science. Springer-Verlag, 2010. To be published.

[7] Iftach Haitner and Thomas Holenstein. On the (im)possibility of key dependent encryption. In Omer Reingold, editor, *Theory of Cryptography, Proceedings of TCC 2009*, number 5444 in Lecture Notes in Computer Science, pages 202–219. Springer-Verlag, 2009.

[8] Dennis Hofheinz and Eike Kiltz. Secure hybrid encryption from weakened key encapsulation. In Alfred Menezes, editor, *Advances in Cryptology, Proceedings of CRYPTO 2007*, number 4622 in Lecture Notes in Computer Science, pages 553–571. Springer-Verlag, 2007.

[9] Dennis Hofheinz and Eike Kiltz. Practical chosen ciphertext secure encryption from factoring. In Antoine Joux, editor, *Advances in Cryptology, Proceedings of EUROCRYPT 2009*, number 5479 in Lecture Notes in Computer Science, pages 313–332. Springer-Verlag, 2009.

[10] Dennis Hofheinz and Dominique Unruh. Towards key-dependent message security in the standard model. In Nigel P. Smart, editor, *Advances in Cryptology, Proceedings of EUROCRYPT 2008*, number 4965 in Lecture Notes in Computer Science, pages 108–126. Springer-Verlag, 2008.

[11] Eike Kiltz and Krzysztof Pietrzak. On the security of padding-based encryption schemes or: Why we cannot prove OAEP secure in the standard model. In Antoine Joux, editor, *Advances in Cryptology, Proceedings of EUROCRYPT 2009*, number 5479 in Lecture Notes in Computer Science, pages 389–406. Springer-Verlag, 2009.

[12] Ronald L. Rivest, Adi Shamir, and Leonard M. Adleman. A method for obtaining digital signatures and public-key cryptosystems. *Communications of the ACM*, 21 (2):120–126, February 1978.

[13] PKCS. *PKCS #1: RSA Encryption Standard, Version 1.5*. RSA Laboratories, 1993.

[14] Peter W. Shor. Algorithms for quantum computation: Discrete logarithms and factoring. In *35th Annual Symposium on Foundations of Computer Science, Proceedings of FOCS 1994*, pages 124–134. IEEE Computer Society, 1994.